THE
HEAVENLY
CITY

ירושלים של מעלה

Menachem Gerlitz

ירושלים של מעלה

THE
HEAVENLY
CITY

Retold from the Hebrew by
SHEINDEL WEINBACH

FELDHEIM PUBLISHERS
Jerusalem • New York • 5739/1979

ISBN 0 87306 147 0
Published 1979

Philipp Feldheim Inc.
96 East Broadway
New York, NY 10002

Feldheim Publishers Ltd
POB 6525 / Jerusalem, Israel

Printed in Israel

Dedicated
to the memory
of all the men and women of vision,
pioneers of the Old Yishuv,
the precious, pure-minded souls of Jerusalem,
who with selfless devotion
bore the years of want and privation
to build the firm spiritual foundations
for the return to life
of the Jewish homeland

Contents

List of Illustrations

Foreword

"The heavenly Jerusalem corresponds directly to the earthly Jerusalem. In His great love of the earthly Jerusalem, He made another in the heavens."

(Midrash Tanchuma, pekudey)

The holiness and uniqueness of Jerusalem did not diminish in the eyes of the Jewish people with the destruction of the Temple and the exile of the nation from their land. In fact, together with their yearning and prayers through the ages for the return of Israel to its land, the eyes of the people were constantly turned to every individual Jew or small group that succeeded in settling in Jerusalem; an aura of glory and holiness accompanied each one who went up to the mountain of God. Moreover, among these few individuals were righteous leaders and great scholars, "giants of spirit" widely known in the diaspora, along with unknown saints who found in the city and its narrow streets a holy society and inspiration — a suitable setting for their worship of God.

Jerusalem of those days was Jerusalem of the world-to-come and not Jerusalem of this world. In the Jerusalem of this world whoever wishes to settle there may do so. In Jerusalem of the world-to-come only those who are invited may come to settle. From the day in 5027 (1267) that Ramban (R. Moshe b. Nachman) renewed the Jewish

11

settlement after the long exile, there followed the steady immigration of individuals, and the influx of groups afterward: the first Chasidim, the students of the Baal Shem Tov in the year 5537 (1777); the students of the Vilna Gaon in the year 5568 (1808); the students of the Chatham Sofer; and afterwards the various immigrations of the 5600s (nineteenth and twentieth centuries). All these were only the souls selected and invited to the holy city.

They left behind them the benefits of the diaspora, rejecting all material goods believed necessary for existence, and came to this city to live a life of the soul, to develop in purity and holiness. Their daily lives were transformed into spirituality, from which we can learn the greatness and beauty of man in his ability to achieve wholeness in character and action. Yet together with this life style they also established, by selflessness and superhuman effort, the basis for the general renewal of Jewish settlement: Torah and welfare institutions, the first neighborhoods — in the beginning within the walled city close to the site of the Temple, and afterwards outside its walls.

The golden age of spirituality for this new Israel was the first half of the century beginning in 5600 (1840-1890). There was hardly an observant writer of those times who did not lift his pen in praise of this renewal, in an attempt to describe the mortal-angels who walked about the holy city. Many non-Jewish writers too found in the Jerusalem of the day inspiration for their literary efforts.

There remains in Jerusalem even today a living miracle: the amazing mixture which came into being when every group that immigrated, each with its own characteristics and ideals, took the best from the other groups and created the well-known personality of the "Yerushalmi" Jew. Apart from the world-embracing wisdom and holiness which have become part of him, he is principally recognized by his humility — for he attributes none of this greatness to himself.

The author does not presume in any way to believe that he has recounted the whole of the story or, for that matter, has succeeded in expressing himself particularly well where others have failed. In fact, these stories were not written originally for the purposes of a book, but as a personal record of the deep impression made upon me while I was engaged in research on the great leaders of Jerusalem, notably Rabbi Yosef Chaim Sonnenfeld, the Rabbi of Jerusalem. Therefore, in some cases incidents may have been mentioned which have relevance only to their times and would seem to have no particular importance in ours, or perhaps in some cases sources have not been entirely checked. However, the emotional gain — the transmission of the deep excitement felt by the author, and the moral content of each story — would justify their being presented as they are. And perhaps in this respect I can say that with the help of God, I have succeeded more than others, and the promise of the book is that between the lines the reader will dream a bit and truly come to feel the beauty and holiness of Jerusalem in those days.

The holiness of the Temple site and of the city of Jerusalem emanates from the indwelling of the sacred spirit. This sacred spirit has never departed and never will leave the holy Temple site and the city. For it is stated "And I shall desolate your sanctuaries," and from this our sages learn that even though they are desolate they are called sanctuaries. So even today Jerusalem maintains its holiness.

ירושלים של מעלה

The Battle
for a Child's
Soul

The Age-Old Deal

ONE couldn't help looking at and wondering about the copper clock with its two huge, heavy bells. Displayed in the shop window in a corner of the old Jewish marketplace in Minsk, its ornate, antique exterior attracted people. But not as much as the very fact of its being up for sale. For, as everyone knew, it was Reb Tuvya Feldsher's clock.

Rumor had it that Reb Tuvya had gone bankrupt and had offered his personal effects up for sale in order to pay his debts. But this rumor was soon quelled. Reb Tuvya had no creditors; he didn't owe any money — and for that matter, never had. He had simply felt the urge, one fine day, to get up and move to Eretz Yisrael. To make his traveling easier, he had decided to sell a large portion of his personal belongings, among which was the copper clock he had inherited from his great-grandfather, the great Rav Avraham Danzig, famous author of *Chayey Adam*.

But even this puzzled the townspeople. What had prompted Reb Tuvya's decision? His business was well established, his Torah-learning fulfilling. Why did he feel a sudden urge to go to a place where destruction was far more evident than renascence? His close friends offered their own theories. Ultimately, despite Reb Tuvya's natural taciturnity, the true reason came out.

His decision dated back to his youth, when he had been called to serve in the Russian army. Then, military service

17

entailed forced labor and a serious danger of forfeiting one's Jewishness. Tuvya swore that if HaShem enabled him to successfully evade the draft, he would settle in Jerusalem and dedicate the rest of his life to Torah study and the service of God. After much effort, Tuvya eventually succeeded in getting himself exempted from service. Family reasons had prevented him from leaving his birthplace at first, and he had put off his vow. When the opportunity finally arrived, he firmly decided not to wait another day.

With tear-filled eyes, the relatives who were remaining behind in Minsk parted from Reb Tuvya as he commenced his daring journey. Summoning the reserves of her failing strength, Reb Tuvya's mother, the famous charity dispenser of Minsk, accompanied her son and his family, her lips continually murmuring the prayer, "May the *Eibershter* watch over you, my dear children." Then Reb Tuvya and his family set out on the long journey to Odessa where they boarded the ship.

Among the other passengers on the ship was a wealthy Vilna Jew, Reb Yona Tabak. Born in Paris to rich, assimilated parents who had long before left the traditions of their people, Yona had come under the influence of Rav Yisrael Lipkin of Salant who, in the course of his efforts to bring Jews close to God, had come to Paris, where he made the acquaintance of the Tabak family. Rav Yisrael had succeeded in convincing the boy to re-embrace Jewish laws and customs. Over the years, Yona had married and moved to Vilna where he absorbed Torah and *yirath shamayim* from various rabbis and teachers. He became an exemplary Jew who meticulously observed simple and difficult mitzvos alike. Material success shone upon him as well, and he amassed much property and many businesses.

Yona Tabak also longed to ascend to Eretz Yisrael to

visit the holy city of Jerusalem and absorb its sacred atmosphere into his fiber. He planned to spend a few weeks in Jerusalem to study the city's unique character and learn about its people and their ways of life.

During his first days on board, Reb Yona's glance fell upon the tall, gaunt form of Reb Tuvya Feldsher, who spent most of the day and even some of the night on deck, surrounded by his many *seforim*. Reb Tuvya immersed himself in Torah study with a marvelous totality, never allowing himself to be dragged into the idle chatter of the other passengers. Reb Yona did not let the young man out of his sight. He often felt driven to go over to the wonderful scholar and engage him in conversation, but he immediately stopped short. What moral right did he have to disturb the single-minded young man from his absorbed study of Torah and draw him into idle chatter?

Vilna was no poor showcase for Torah scholars, and Reb Yona had indeed heard and seen many before. What was it then that attracted the rich merchant to this man? Was it some special charm Reb Tuvya exuded? Was the fiber from which great souls are made woven into his expression? By the third day out at sea, Reb Yona could restrain himself no longer. His curiosity overcame his sense of propriety and he approached the young man, casually asking him about his health and the purpose of his journey to Eretz Yisrael. Reb Tuvya obliged by telling his co-traveler that he was bound for Jerusalem in order to settle there.

"And what will you do for a livelihood?" asked Reb Yona.

"Oh, I have a rich Father," was the confident reply.

"Where is he?"

"Tell me where He isn't! The entire earth is full of His glory. . ."

Reb Yona met Reb Tuvya's family, and he posed the same question to Reb Tuvya's wife, Tzirel.

"Livelihood is no problem," she retorted with marvelous coolness. "My dear husband will sit and study Torah, and I am sure that God will mercifully aid His children."

"And if indeed the need arises," she added as a practical afterthought, "I can always find something to do to help out. The main thing is that my husband continue his studies."

A warm friendship sprang up between the two men, which, having once cemented itself, continued to grow from day to day. Reb Yona's estimation of his new friend expressed itself tangibly in a climactic scene that took place as they approached the shoreline, only three hours away from the holy land. The captain had announced that very soon their feet would tread upon the ground of their beloved homeland. Upon this announcement, Reb Yona called Reb Tuvya to his cabin for a talk.

"I have a deal to offer you," he stated. "You, Reb Tuvya, will sit and immerse yourself in study, confident of your source of income. I, on the other hand, will supply you with a monthly stipend which will adequately cover all your expenses, just like the age-old agreement that was drawn up between Yissachar and Zevulun."

Completely caught by surprise, Reb Tuvya was speechless at first. Such a possibility had never entered his mind! Reb Yona realized that the decision was certainly not one that could or should be made on the spot. It needed contemplation and time, and so Reb Yona gave his friend two days to come to a decision.

Just as they finished talking, the sound of the ship's foghorn reached their ears together with the noise of great scrambling on the upper deck. They had arrived at Jaffa port, and the passengers disembarked. Swept along with the human tide, Reb Tuvya and Reb Yona shortly found themselves on holy ground. Overcome with emotion, they stooped to kiss the rocky terrain, not forgetting in their excitement to thank the One Who had made this dream-realization possible.

Reb Tuvya remained kneeling on the heavenly earth a long time, wrapped up in many thoughts and emotions. Finally, Reb Yona reminded him that they had not yet reached their final destination and that plans for the remainder of the trip must still be made. Having been thus brought back to the present and its problems, Reb Tuvya took stock of his family and belongings, hired donkeys to transport them, and they were on their way to Jerusalem.

As soon as they were en route again, Reb Yona once more reminded Reb Tuvya of his proposal. "I want you to come to a speedy decision," he urged. "My business affairs only allow me a few days here and I would like to have a definite answer before I leave."

Tzirel Feldsher had already been informed of the proposal, and she now responded to Yona's remarks. "Your suggestion requires a great deal of thought. A decision in such weighty matters, upon which heavenly and earthly worlds depend, needs thorough contemplation. We cannot arrive at a speedy decision." Reb Yona, not intimidated in the least by her resoluteness, still insisted that the matter be settled before his departure.

In the end they decided to bring the matter before Rav Shmuel Salant, the Rav of Jerusalem, whose fame had spread to Europe. They would attempt to find some solution through his wise efforts.

At the appointed time, on the morrow, Reb Tuvya and his helpmate Tzirel appeared at Rav Shmuel's home, followed shortly by Reb Yona Tabak.

Rav Shmuel's advancing age was evidenced by his near blindness and his semi-reclining position. He sat on a stuffed chair and offered his hand to Reb Yona and to Reb Tuvya in greeting and then turned his attention to the subject at hand. Reb Yona, who had the floor first, explained and elaborated upon how his business affairs left him with a bare minimum of time for Torah study. On the other hand, Reb Tuvya, whom he had befriended aboard ship, had all of his time to dedicate to Torah study but had no means of supporting himself and assuring his continued study. "And so you see," he concluded logically, "that under these circumstances, my offer to Reb Tuvya is a perfect opportunity all around." And he solicited the Rav's aid in actualizing his practical idea.

"And what is your opinion of this proposition?" the Rav turned to Reb Tuvya. "Can you think of a better deal?"

"It truly sounds ideal, but she is still opposed to it," answered Reb Tuva with a nod in the direction of his wife. "She does not approve of this deal one bit."

"And why should you disagree?" the Rov asked Tzirel.

"I resent the fact that my husband, who spends his days and nights in Torah study, should forfeit half of his portion in *olam haba* for a bribe," she exclaimed vehemently. "Torah is not merchandise that one can trade or barter or dispose of as one pleases. I don't want my husband to sell even the smallest share of his Torah and good deeds..."

Rav Shmuel patiently heard her out. Then he began to calm the excited woman. "Who says that you have to divide your reward and give it away? The Holy One, blessed is He, has enough and to spare for everyone — Yissachar and Zevulun both. Neither must forfeit any part of his share to the other."

Rav Shmuel went even further. He suggested, "If you still fear for your *olam haba* and want added security,

Rav Shmuel Salant

General view of the Old City

you may draw up a contract between the two parties which can be properly signed and witnessed." The words were no sooner out of his mouth than the Rav's *shamash* had ready a feather pen, an inkwell, and a clean sheet of paper. The contract was drawn up, and both men signed it.

Explicitly stated in the last paragraph of the document was a clause Rav Shmuel had dictated, "The reward designated for Reb Tuvya in *olam haba* will not be diminished by a single iota..."

"May God bless this venture with success," the Rav wished them heartily as he shook both partners' hands. He then placed the signed contract in a desk drawer for safekeeping.

Shoemaker and Tzaddik

IT IS COMMONPLACE ENOUGH for a Jew to bring his troubles, his problems, his heavy heart, to a wise man and beg that he pray for him. Haven't Jews in every age and clime brought their sorrowful souls to *tzaddikim* in the fervent hope that the pure, sterling cry of an untainted soul would pierce the heavens and attain action?

Like connective tissue in the body, like a bridge spanning opposite banks, like a funnel channeling blessings from above, so does the *tzaddik* serve his brothers. In times of danger and trouble, in drought, hunger, or plague, the *tzaddik* seeks help from above through the power of his prayer and subverts the evil decree. Our Sages' pronouncement, "A *tzaddik* decrees and God fulfills," has been demonstrated time and again to Jewish communities throughout history. And if Reb Tuvya ever doubted this axiom, he was convinced of its truth after one week's residence in Jerusalem. A remarkable incident left an indelible impression upon him.

The long and arduous journey from Minsk to Odessa had taken its toll on Reb Tuvya's shoes. After only four days' sojourn in Jerusalem, he found it necessary to visit a shoemaker. Reb Nissan's workshop, situated in one of the alleys behind the Batrak *shuk,* was so dark and cramped and almost impossible to find that it might have been described as little more than a hole-in-the-wall.

But when he finally did find it, Reb Tuvya was cordially invited to sit down and wait while the shoemaker performed the necessary repair. He crouched, found himself a low stool, removed his shoes, and waited patiently.

In the span of five seconds a spry visitor was in and out of the shop, leaving behind him on Reb Nissan's worktable a small, folded note. The visitor? The well-known octogenarian Reb Azriel. The note? Well, a note. It happened so suddenly that Reb Tuvya thought that the shoemaker, bent intently over his work, had not noticed the intruder. A breeze stirred up by the old man's swift exit wafted the slip of paper aloft and allowed Reb Tuvya a peek at its contents. "Pray for my grandson, Elchanan ben Zlata, that he follow the true path," it read.

A shoemaker and sayer of prayers! Can one encompass both occupations? marveled Reb Tuvya. The concept of a secret *tzaddik* was not strange to Reb Tuvya, who had heard of them in Minsk. These were people who wore the garment of simplicity; they plied commonplace professions and trades, but they constantly mouthed holy words of study, day and night. They would not move four cubits without their *tefillin*. Reb Tuvya remembered all he had heard about Reb Itzele, who never slept more than two hours a night, and about Reb Ozer Ginz — also a Minsker Jew — who secretly provided for impoverished widows and the marriage of poor orphans. Such *tzaddikim* fit the image Reb Tuvya had of *tzaddikim nistarim*. But this shoemaker, at his worktable all day without *tefillin*, seemed no more than than a common laborer.

Maybe, reflected Reb Tuvya, *Reb Azriel has erred. Perhaps his advanced age causes the old man to ignore all the tzaddikim and wise men of this city and beg a shoemaker to pray for him?*

What! Reb Azriel senile? Reb Tuvya retracted his former thought. *It cannot be! Not at all! Why, it was only yesterday that I heard him exchanging views with the famous Rav Shneyur Zalman of Lublin on the halachic problems of* traifoth *and he did so with unsurpassable genius. What then does this all mean?*

Reb Tuvya sat in the small cubbyhole of a store, puzzling at the enigma until the shoemaker handed him the mended shoes. He paid and rose to make way for future customers, without being any the wiser.

Seeking a Room and Finding a Friend

FULLY SHOD, Reb Tuvya went forth to complete his arrangements, chief among which was the need for a suitable apartment. Not living quarters — those he had found without exertion in the main street of the Jewish quarter. Actually, in those days there was no problem of living space, either in the old city or in the new one which was progressively growing. No one could say that he had sought an apartment and not found one. Not only was Reb Tuvya's new home situated in excellent surroundings, but it adjoined the courtyard of Reb Leib ben Moshe Chayim who was rated among the great men of Jerusalem. Reb Tuvya's living quarters were truly enviable.

What then was Reb Tuvya looking for? Not living quarters but a place where he could have privacy, a room where he could sit and study, undisturbed by the outside world. The first specification for this meditation room, as one might call it, was that it should be near Rav Shmuel Salant. Reb Tuvya wanted the assurance that if any difficulty arose in the course of his Torah study he would not have far to go to have his problem solved.

Such an ideal room actually did exist, and it was vacant as well. Situated in the courtyard of Rabbi Yehuda Ha-Chasid's Churva synagogue, it was right by Rav Shmuel's home. The snag was that such prime real estate, though barely large enough to contain a table and chair, had at least one other prospective customer besides Reb Tuvya, a customer who had more of a claim on it than he. In fact, Reb Tuvya's chances were quite slim.

"HaChurva" — Rabbi Yehuda haChasid Synagogue

*Interior view of the Churva
Synagogue — the holy ark*

This room had formerly belonged to the *rosh yeshiva* of
Yeshivath Etz Chayim, the famous Rav Eliezer (Leizer)
Dan Ralbag. Within its solitary four walls he had com-
posed the Torah lectures he delivered to the yeshiva
students. Now, after Rav Leizer Dan's death, the room
remained vacant, waiting for the lucky man who would
merit it next. As there were many candidates, the neighborhood committee left the whole matter to Rav Shmuel
Salant's discretion.

High up on the list was Reb Simcha Polnoa, one of the
choice scholars of the yeshiva, a prodigiously tireless *mathmid* and a truly Godfearing man who was beloved by all.
These qualities made Reb Simcha the generally-favored
candidate. Besides his popularity, he had another factor
going for him; Reb Simcha had had his eyes on this room
still in Rav Leizer Dan's lifetime. In fact, when Rav Leizer
Dan was away lecturing to the students in the yeshiva,
Reb Simcha would sneak in, lock the door tightly upon
its ancient lock, and spend glorious hours in utter solitude,
deeply immersed in profitable study. As soon as he heard
Rav Leizer Dan's footsteps descending the stairs to the
courtyard, he would slip out and away as quietly as he
had come, without anyone but he being the wiser for it.
Now Reb Simcha felt that he had a valid and concrete
claim upon the room that he had already used so many
times.

But a man like Reb Tuvya is not easily discouraged.
One fine day he went directly to Rav Shmuel and plainly
stated his request. Even his good wife Tzirel did her bit
by accompanying Tuvya and explaining, volubly and
pungently, how impossible it was for her husband to study
at home with the little children running around underfoot
and disturbing his peace of mind.

Reb Simcha got word of this visit and immediately determined that he would not give up 'his' room without a good fight. Although not exactly thought a man of action by his companions, he rushed home and prodded his wife to make herself presentable and proceed directly to Rav Shmuel's home. The children were deposited at helpful if curious neighbors, his wife's kerchief was set to rights and her apron smoothed down — and the battle was on.

When his wife had left to plead her husband's cause, Reb Simcha posted himself vigilantly in a corner of the house to do his share. He had already dropped eighteen coins into the "Rabbi Mai'ir Baal HaNess" *pushka* and he now began to pray with all his might for his wife's success. He looked forward with *bitachon* to victory.

Meanwhile, the battle raged fiercely in the Rav's home. The "advocates" argued their causes as best they could, and Rav Shmuel had the task of negotiating a just and equitable peace for these two *talmidey chachamim*. What was he to do?

The women finished their arguments and waited silently and respectfully, and not a little hopefully, for the decision of their eminent judge. Rav Shmuel sat deep in thought for some time. Then, apparently having reached a decision, he bade his *shamash* fetch Reb Simcha. The two parties waited tensely until Reb Simcha appeared, at which point Rav Shmuel stood up and spoke decisively, "I have heard the arguments of both sides. Chazal teach that one should not study Torah all alone. I therefore strongly advise you both, Reb Simcha and Reb Tuvya, to join forces and study together in the disputed room. Together you will attain perfection in Torah and in character. And so," he exclaimed, "the room belongs to both of you!"

Tears sprang forth simultaneously from the eyes of Reb Simcha and Reb Tuvya — tears of joy and brotherhood.

Profitable Jealousy

"MINCHA! MINCHA!" cried Dayan Moshe Nachum Wallenstein early one Friday afternoon of a Jerusalem winter. Standing in the courtyard of the Churva synagogue, he had been trying for some time now to assemble a *minyon* for early *mincha* but still lacked three Jews.

Chaikel, the *shamash* of the Churva synagogue, heard the call but was not free to answer it. He had too many things to do on this short *erev*-Shabbath. He still had to dust the entire interior of the large *shul,* to prepare the wicks and set them in the huge chandeliers, to spread white cloths upon the tables and to light dozens of kerosene lamps, all in honor of Shabbath. Chaikel was accustomed to praying *mincha* after candle-lighting, together with the congregants. Why should he make an exception today?

Chaikel lugged the heavy ladder to the Torah ark and laboriously hoisted his bulky frame up its rungs. He carefully removed the enormous graying weekday curtain and substituted the white silk Shabbath *parocheth*, rose and gold embroidered, which proudly bore the inscription, "Donated to the Churva *shul* by Yehudith, the wife of the *oheiv* Yisrael, Sir Moses Montefiore, upon her visit to Jerusalem."

Chaikel lovingly read the words, "In honor of Shabbath and in honor of the Torah," feeling the special aura of that holy day as it approached. His eyes glistened with love and emotion.

Rabbi
Simcha Polnoa

Chaikel, the shamash of the Churva Synagogue

His reveries were sharply broken by a harsh knock on the eastern window. "Chaikel! Chaikel!" someone was calling. The efficient *shamash* turned toward the sound and saw none other than the eminent Rav Moshe Nachum summoning him to interrupt his labors and come join the *minyan*. With proper respect for a *talmid chacham*, Chaikel hurried down the ladder, donned his frock-coat and joined the seven men outside in the old Menachem Tziyon *shul*. Seeing that they still lacked two men for the *minyan*, he looked significantly at Reb Moshe Nochum and then glanced just as significantly at the room in the courtyard which belonged to, and presently contained, Reb Simcha Polnoa and Reb Tuvya Feldsher.

Chaikel was not used to sparing words. Always ready with some spicy comment, personal insight or sharp remark about any bit of news that came his way, Chaikel did not now spare the world — that is the other seven *minyan*-makers — his opinion of Rav Shmuel's *shidduch*. He had grave doubts about the lasting quality of the union of the strange pair. "And why, after all, should we fool ourselves," he predicted with a half-smile. "Reb Simcha Polnoa stems from a renowned chassidic background. Thick chassidic blood courses through his veins. He claims to be the greatgrandson of Rav Yaakov Yoseif of Polnoa, one of the Ba'al Shem Tov's leading disciples and author of *Toldoth Yaakov Yoseif*. Reb Simcha himself is thorougly immersed in the wellsprings of *chassiduth*. They say that his table is one continuous forum for chassidic tales. And despite his tremendous devotion to Torah-study, he still manages to spend hours upon hours on Shabbaths and Yamim Tovim at Rav El'azar Mendel Biderman's*

---

*Rav El'azar Menachem Mendel, son of Rav Moshe, was Lelover Rebbe from 5611 (1851) to 5643 (1883).

tish, where he is the happiest of human beings if he suc-
ceeds in grabbing some crumbs of the *rebbe's* holy *shirayim*
(leftovers) to bring home to his wife and children. If
fortune truly smiles upon him, and the *rebbe* honors him
with a request for a Shabbath *zemer* — then he floats in
seventh heaven.

"Now, on the other hand, you have Reb Tuvya Feldsher.
A different breed altogether. Born and bred a Litvack, as
far from *chassiduth* as a rifle's shot, he is steeped in the
ways and customs of the Vilna Gaon. In addition to all
this he is a serious man by nature, wrapped up in himself,
solitary and self-contained. He weighs his words before
they leave his mouth, a mouth which is never graced by
the hint of a smile. Now how can you expect such a
'couple' to live in harmony?" Chaikel summed up.

Chaikel could have harangued on and on were it not
for a singular interruption. To everyone's astonishment,
the door of the tiny room in the courtyard opened to emit
Reb Tuvya and Reb Simcha, both aglow with the inner
and outer holiness bestowed by the approaching Shabbath,
both come to complete Rav Moshe Nachum's early *mincha*
as its ninth and tenth men.

The *chazan* began *mincha* right away, but not before
someone took a crack at Chaikel's character analysis, "Nu,
what do you say now to the *shidduch*? Look at the happy
pair for yourself!" Chaikel was thwacked heartily and a
bit painfully on the back, but it was his pride that hurt
most. Not being in the mood to argue after such a blow
to both, he threw himself earnestly into his davening and
then went back, considerably subdued, to his *erev*-Shabbath
labors.

Actually Chaikel's assertion was groundless. Rav
Shmuel's match was an especially suitable one. Reb Simcha
was never repelled by Reb Tuvya's cold, clinical, Lithu-

anian approach; Reb Tuvya was never burned by Reb Simcha's fiery chassidic enthusiasm. The love of Torah both harbored in their hearts tempered them and united them in brotherhood to such a visible extent, that their companions in Etz Chayim yeshiva called them David and Yonathan. Reb Simcha would even admit jokingly that without his friend, Reb Tuvya, he felt himself half a person. The two had come to a secret agreement upon three points: to fully fulfill the command of loving one's friend as oneself in respect to one another, to study Torah for its own sake — to the best of their ability — within their room all day and part of the night, and never to speak idle talk within the walls of their beloved chamber.

Such a strong bond of friendship could not avoid arousing the envy of the other scholars of the yeshiva. This feeling was shared by anyone who chanced to pass by outside the high window of the tiny room and overhear the sweet sounds of Torah escaping from within.

The envy directed against this happy pair was overt, yet strangely enough, a covert jealousy penetrated Reb Tuvya's pure heart. At first it was a mere subconscious twinge, of which he himself was unaware. Jealousy was a feeling that Reb Tuvya had never harbored against his fellowman, yet now he found it occupying a definite share of his emotions. He was actually jealous of his dedicated friend, Reb Simcha. Reb Tuvya tried desperately to uproot this insidious envy, to extract it completely, but the more he increased his efforts, to choke off this envy, the more it took root and worked its way into his consciousness.

What actually was there about Reb Simcha to envy? A man who owned nothing, who managed to survive somehow from the bare pittance he received each month from the yeshiva. Anyone who chanced to pay a visit to his attic room, one of the many such humble dwellings in the neighborhood of the Dung Gate, found it on the verge of collapse. Cramped, dark, and moldy, boasting a few sticks of old furniture, the single room housed Reb Simcha, his eight children, and his wife who slaved from morning to night to keep her children fed and clothed. The brown paper stuck over the broken windowpanes kept the more bitter winds from entering during the biting Jerusalem winters. Surely there was nothing here for Reb Tuvya to envy! Such conditions could evoke only compassion in any human breast!

As for Reb Tuvya's living conditions, they were completely different. His was a comfortable apartment with everything always in its proper place. His well-dressed children never had a torn sock or loose button. Tzirel could afford to, and gladly did, give any article of clothing that began to show signs of wear to less fortunate neighbors, who accepted her gifts eagerly. Tuvya's monthly stipend was the generous allotment that wealthy Reb Yona Tabak sent faithfully, in fulfillment of his sacred promise, month in and month out. He didn't have to rely on the yeshiva's meager handout.

What then was this envy that gnawed away at pious Reb Tuvya?

Involved in most of what transpired in his constituency, Rav Shmuel Salant was unknowingly responsible for the conflict that raged within Reb Tuvya. It was customary on Shavuoth for the yeshiva disciples to visit the old Rav who was also the Rosh haYeshiva, and wish him "Good Yom Tov" at which time Rav Shmuel would deliver his annual Shavuoth lecture. It was on this occasion that Reb Tuvya was suddenly faced with the upsetting realization that his friend was much closer to everlasting fulfillment than he was.

That particular Shavuoth happened to fall upon a Friday and so Rav Shmuel limited his usually lengthy *drasha*. But apparently its impact was not diminished by its brevity. If anything, it was heightened.

The message was based upon a *Midrash Rabba* and, as Rav Shmuel spoke, an intense silence descended upon his listeners. Every precious word was invested with deep meanings, as his clear, ringing voice cut the stillness and was swallowed up into the listening ears and hearts of the men seated around the table.

"The story is told of Rabbi Shimon ben Chalafta who came home one Friday to find his house bare. Shabbath was approaching but he had nothing with which to enjoy it. What did he do? He went to the outskirts of the city to pour out his heart to God. His prayers ascended to the heavenly throne itself where they were accepted and Rabbi Shimon was given a precious stone which he hurried to redeem. The considerable sum of money which he received enabled him to buy lavishly for the coming Shabbath. When he brought his bounty home, he was greeted by a questioning wife, 'Where did all this come from?' she wanted to know. Rabbi Shimon explained that it had been provided by a heavenly hand. She then threatened not to taste a morsel unless he returned the entire sum after Shabbath. When Rabbi Shimon inquired what her reasons were she replied, 'Do you want your table in Gan Eiden to be lacking while your colleague's tables are replete?' Rabbi Shimon went to Rabbi (Rabbi Yehuda HaNassi) and told him the story. Rabbi told him to reassure his wife that he, Rabbi, would guarantee to replenish any spiritual lack of theirs from his own table in *olam haba*. When Rabbi Shimon duly went and informed her of Rabbi's words, she demanded to be brought to the great man that she might answer him personally. 'Does one man see another in the

the world to come?' she asked him. 'Does not each *tzaddik* exist separately, as it is written in *Koheleth* 12, "For a man goes to his world..." The verse states "*his world*" and not "*his worlds.*" From here we learn that in the world to come each man is for himself.' Thereupon her husband went and returned the gem."

The yeshiva scholars listened while Rav Shmuel explained the midrash:

"The midrash does not reveal to us what answer Rabbi gave to Rabbi Shimon's wife, but apparently her words affected him deeply. Rabbi Shimon, as well, had no final reply to his wife's argument and returned the gem to its heavenly source. What significance lay in her words that they were able to silence the very Prince of Israel?" posed the Rav of Jerusalem. "Even if each tzaddik *is* separated from his fellow tzaddikim in the world to come, could not Rabbi — who testified before his death that he did not physically enjoy this world even to the extent of his smallest finger — could this phenomenal tzaddik not find a medium of exchange with which to compensate Rabbi Shimon in *olam haba* for the deficiency in his portion as a result of the gem that he had enjoyed upon this world?"

Rav Shmuel went on to dispose of his own question: "Rabbi Shimon's wife wished to intimate in her words that Rabbi could not compensate her husband in the world-to-come. Truly, Rabbi's position in the world of truth would be considerable, but all the treasures that awaited him there would not be of the same currency as that in which Rabbi Shimon would be paid. There would be no medium of exchanging the treasure of one for the treasure the other was lacking. Rabbi Shimon had studied Torah all his days, under the trying conditions of hardship and deprivation, as opposed to Rabbi, whose Torah-study was pursued under favorable circumstances of wealth and comfort. How could Rabbi repay from his share what was lacking from Rabbi Shimon's share, when it involved a totally different medium of exchange? Rabbi realized the validity of the woman's argument, as did her husband, and they both bowed to her plea that the gem be returned."

Rav Shmuel served his guests some wine for a *l'chayim*, and then they all went their separate ways, greatly elevated by what they had just heard. Rav Shmuel had hit the mark with his timely words. The yeshiva treasury had been hit badly; outside income trickled in by drops, and the prognosis was depressing. The yeshiva treasurers had managed to arrange a loan before Yom Tov to distribute to the scholars on account, but they needed this additional encouragement from Rav Shmuel who had wisely chosen the subject of his Shavuoth message. Returning to their homes the scholars of Jerusalem had fare to offer on their Yom Tov tables — spiritual fare rather than Shavuoth cheesecake and delicacies. They served up Rav Shmuel's reassuring message that those who studied Torah under conditions of want and deprivation were truly great, and their reward was beyond all measure. Their families savored this fare, and it somehow filled their empty bellies as well as their hearts.

There was one person, however, who took the message personally, and it cut as deeply as a knife thrust. He was the only one to whom the Rav's message did not apply, yet, by that very fact, it applied all the more. Reb Tuvya with his fat monthly check did not belong in the same class as the yeshiva students who had to break their heads to make ends meet. And when they didn't succeed in making ends meet, which was rather too often, they had to break their heads to find loans to tide them over the next check. Reb Tuvya's monthly stipend provided a plentiful

Shabbath table for his family, enabled him to pay his son's *cheider* tuition on time, and would probably have sufficed to pay the living expenses of three or four yeshiva families. It left him with a clear head, unburdened shoulders, and the freedom to concentrate all of his efforts on his study.

"But," thought Reb Tuvya introspectively, "the Rav stressed the value of Torah study under conditions of want and deprivation. Why am I 'punished' by having it so easy, by having my Torah served up to me on a silver platter?" He was convinced that his wealth made him less worthy than his good friend Reb Simcha and the other yeshiva scholars.

Reb Tuvya, by nature a taciturn man, kept his burden to himself. Neither his wife nor his best friend Reb Simcha ever heard the slightest sigh of discontent leave his lips, despite the hurt that gnawed and grew within him. But his silence did not preclude his devising plans to 'rid' himself of his good fortune by breaking with his partner, Reb Yona Tabak.

Although she never heard any tangible expression of her husband's disquietude, Tzirel intuitively felt that something distressed him. Too sensitive to ask him directly, she nevertheless noted his pinched look and pale face, which she knew did not result from inadequate diet. In vain did she try to hint delicately that he tell her what might be bothering him. He kept his mental anguish deeply hidden.

It is quite possible that Reb Tuvya's pain might have petered down to a twinge with the healing balm of passing time. The midrash he had heard from Rav Shmuel would have filtered down to his subconscious to appear only upon rare occasions. Possible and probable, but not destined to be so. Providence willed that Reb Tuvya should not forget that his lot of plenty differed from the lot of poverty shared by his peers.

The seed planted innocently by Rav Shmuel did not, in fact, rest forgotten in the dark, but germinated and took root soon after its initial planting on Shavuoth. Two days later, in the late evening, Reb Tuvya and his learning-mate, Reb Simcha, were interrupted from their Torah study by a frantic knocking on the window of their tiny room. It was Chaikel the *shamash,* telling them to go out and accompany their Rav.

Where was the elderly Rav Shmuel going at this time of night? Where were all of his *talmidim* going, equipped with lanterns? Who in Jerusalem could see Rav Shmuel going somewhere and not accompany him? And so the twosome joined the growing throng of *talmidim* and towns-folk in a solemn procession which they quickly discovered to be a funeral. Reb Sheima Slonim, renowned Etz Cha-yim scholar of forty-two, had died a sudden death in his Batey Machseh home just before evening. True to the custom of Jerusalem, he was being brought to his eternal rest before the next day dawned.

By the time the procession led by Rav Shmuel reached Batey Machseh, the purification of the body had already been completed. Nevertheless, the funeral did not proceed. Whispered conjectures flying from ear to mouth had it that they were waiting for the Brisker Rav, Rav Yehoshua Leib Diskin, to make his appearance. Since that *tzaddik* rarely ventured out, the family felt that his presence would lend unexpected prestige to Reb Sheima's last voyage, and had requested that the assemblage wait until he arrived.

No one really knew why the Brisker Rav had made an exception this time. He hardly ever attended funerals. As a matter of fact, he rarely left his home at all. Why did Reb Sheima merit this unusual show of respect?

Rav Yehoshua Leib doubtlessly knew the deceased and appreciated the greatness of his soul, or so the public conjectured. That was why he would come forth to pay his last respects. Some of the men, however, ventured to doubt that Rav Yehoshua Leib would come. The murmuring crowd threw this question around and looked at its different angles, but suddenly the murmurs were hushed and complete silence reigned. The counterargument no longer had any force behind it, for Rav Yehoshua Leib had arrived, accompanied by Rav Yosef Chayim Sonnenfeld. A sign was given for the breaking of a sherd and the covered bier was lifted by the crowd of mourners.

The stillness was then broken by the thundering voice of Rav Yitzchak Winograd, the *rosh yeshiva* of Yeshiva Torath Chayim, who spoke at the request of his *rebbe,* the Brisker Rav. His words cut through the silence of the night and captured the tense hearts of his listeners. "Oy!" he cried out. "Alas! We have lost Reb Sheima, who studied Torah himself and propagated it among others, Torah studied in poverty and through straits..." His voice broke off with emotion, but he then continued with renewed strength. "Ahhh... Even while the members of his house hungered for bread, Reb Sheima did not cease his constant study..."

Tears streamed unashamedly from more than a thousand pairs of eyes. No heart was untouched by the loss of this precious Jew.

The procession began to move forward, toward Har haZeithim. Solemnly bringing up the rear, the Brisker Rav accompanied the mourners, bent over and deep in sorrow, until the last man had left the city gates and the deceased was laid to rest. It was midnight when the final clod of earth was carefully thrown over the pure remains of the saintly Reb Sheima, and the citizens of Jerusalem were able to return to their homes to catch a few hours of sleep before day broke.

שיבת תורת חיים הכללית

The building of Yeshivath Torath Chayim

Why did Reb Sheima merit the Brisker Rav's presence at his funeral? Reb Tuvya wondered as he made his way home. His ears still rang with the forceful words of Rav Yitzchak Winograd, "Torah studied in poverty and through straits..." Reb Tuvya prepared himself for sleep, recited the Shma, and threw himself angrily upon his bed. But sleep, instead of coming, seemed to purposely evade him. His mind buzzed. His ears rang. His eyes blazed. He relived the funeral with the brief stirring words of eulogy, and saw the form of the saintly Brisker Rav poised beside the crowd. He saw the covered form of the deceased who had merited such exceptional honor. And again he heard the words ringing out in the stillness of the thousand listening people, "Torah studied in poverty and through straits..." The scene repeated itself over and over, robbing him of sleep and draining his energy. Two hours of tossing and turning convinced Reb Tuvya that sleep would not visit him that night. Bleary-eyed, he left his comfortless bed, and after washing his hands and lighting a candle, he removed a *seifer* from one of the shelves with trembling but cautious hands, in order not to awaken the sleeping members of his household. Maybe through study he would be rewarded with rejuvenating sleep.

As Providence would have it, Reb Tuvya opened the *Midrash Rabba* he had randomly chosen to the *sedra* of Pekudey where the Midrash told of Rabbi Shimon and his precious gem. Rav Shmuel's words jumped out at him, and the scene of the *talmidim* seated at their rosh yeshiva's Shavuoth table filled the panorama of his mind's eye. "Ahh!" a sigh escaped him involuntarily, "Torah studied in poverty! Torah studied through suffering! How dear such Torah study is in the eyes of HaShem. When shall I, too, be able to achieve it? When, oh when?" he agonized, and sighing deeply, he finally fell, through sheer exhaustion, into a tortured sleep.

Reb Daniyel Beregsas Interprets a Dream

AN OCCASIONAL ROOSTER vociferously greeted the dawn here and there, but Jerusalem still had its eyes shuttered and was catching another forty winks before it welcomed the approaching sunburst of morning.

With his usual vim and vigor, Reb Simcha tapped on the window, ready to greet the new day as always with early-morning *vathikin* prayers. Reb Tuvya awoke bathed with sweat, relieved to be released from the nightmares that had visited him throughout his bare hour-and-a-half of restless sleep. He was thoroughly exhausted but quickly pulled himself together, arising like a lion from where he had fallen asleep over his *seifer*. After making the necessary preparations, he speedily joined his friend outside.

Reb Tuvya davened as usual, following his morning prayers with the lesson in *mussar* that he and Reb Simcha never missed. After these essentials had been disposed of, he approached three men who had remained in *shul,* asking them to act as a *beith din* to make good his dreams of the night before. The three, among them Reb Simcha, seated themselves as a *beith din.*

Reb Simcha, true to his name, was a cheerful person, undaunted by the harshest of circumstances. He greeted life and whatever it had in store for him with a merry chassidic *niggun* on his lips or under his breath, and his *niggun* would dispel all black clouds. Consequently, he couldn't bear to see anyone else distressed, and he now begged Reb Tuvya to relate his dream so that he might swiftly break the hold it had over his friend.

"It was a whole conglomeration of dreams, may God preserve us," the latter intoned in gloomy contrast to Reb Simcha's cheery tones. "They were all so intertwined and confused that I can't even recall them myself. I think I saw Shir haShirim and Iyov and more..."

At these words Reb Simcha literally jumped for joy. "You saw Shir haShirim? Do you recall what our Sages say about that? 'He who sees Shir haShirim in a dream is ready for *chassiduth*.' If so, my dear friend, there is truly some hope for you. The cold Litvak will, in the end, be transformed into a *chassid*. That is the interpretation of your dream, no more and no less."

"No!" Reb Tuvya rejected this one-sided prophecy, lapsing into deeper melancholy. "It was not the *saifer* that I saw, it was only random verses and half-verses. I saw, for example, the *pasuk*, 'I am black and beautiful,' and 'A thousand to you, Shlomo, and two hundred...' I could find no way to relate to them, they had no meaning for me personally."

Of the few remaining Jews in *shul* there was one who was an expert in *midrashim*. Reb Daniyel Beregsas, the *shul's* oldest and most respected worshiper, occupying his usual place by the bookcase, overheard the previous conversation. "Your dream may have hinted at our Sages' comment on the verse 'A thousand to you, Shlomo,'" he nodded wisely.

"What comment?" Reb Tuvya walked over to the venerable Reb Daniyel and leaned over to hear him distinctly.

"The thousand mentioned in the *pasuk*," the nonagenarian explained to his eager listener, "alludes to Naftali, who studied Torah in poverty, while the two hundred

47

mentioned next refers to Yissachar, who studied Torah while being supported by Zevulun."

Reb Daniyel had no way of gauging what deep effect his simple words would have upon Reb Tuvya. Wrapped up in his world of study, and rarely leaving his corner by the bookcase in the *shul,* the old man did not understand Reb Tuvya's sensitive soul enough to know that his words had shot through the younger man like a bolt of lightning. And Reb Tuvya, thoroughly confused from a sleepless night full of perplexing dreams, stood there as if the floor had given way beneath his trembling feet. How had Reb Daniyel known that he had been bothered by this exact dilemma — that of studying Torah like Yissachar, while his peers were accumulating Torah like Naftali at a five-fold rate? While he studied in comfort, they studied in destitution, and their Torah was worth so much more.

How had this old man, who had never exchanged half a dozen words with Reb Tuvya before, known how to strike at his core? With the mere breath of his lips, Reb Daniyel had destroyed Reb Tuvya's peace, smashed his very world. Rav Shmuel Salant had struck the first blow, Reb Yitzchak Winograd had undermined the foundation, and now Reb Daniyel had completed the wrecking.

The three members of Reb Tuvya's *beith din* did their best to lend favorable interpretations to his dreams, but they could not dispel the heavy, black clouds of despair that possessed him during his waking hours. Thoroughly confused and depressed, Reb Tuvya made his tortured way home while he grappled inwardly with his problem. *Why did the Omniscient Provider devise all these events to befall me in such rapid sequence? Does He truly wish me to break my partnership with my earthly provider, Yona Tabak? Should I relinquish this opportunity of lifetime security in favor of eking out some kind of existence from the monthly apology of a subsidy from the yeshiva? Or is all this a scheme of some evil spirits, sent to test and temper me? What if I am not able, in the end, to withstand the trials of poverty? Will I have then thrown all my chances for a Torah-future to the winds, to be left altogether emptyhanded? How am I to know what to do, what to choose, what to think? Oy, who can help me out of this terrible dilemma?*

Just as he was approaching home, his small son Azriel rushed up to his father with what he considered good news. "A letter came, Tatta, from Uncle Yona." Little Azriel had often heard the name Yona Tabak mentioned at home in grateful tones. "Hurry, and see what it says," he urged. "Read the good news for yourself."

Reb Tuvya entered his house and was handed the letter. Its message was brief:

> Having been informed of the difficult year that this has been for the people of Jerusalem due to the lack of rains and the resulting scarcity of food, I am taking the initiative of doubling your monthly check so that you may continue to study Torah undisturbed by financial worries.
>
> Sincerely and respectfully,
Yona Tabak

Tzirel's face beamed as the words were read to her. The total lack of rain that entire winter had had terrible repercussions throughout the city. Food and water were both scarce and the little that was available was priced sky-high. *Reb Yona Tabak is a wise and good man,* she thought gratefully, looking at her husband to see whether his reaction matched hers. But Reb Tuvya took the news with a grim countenance. The lines in his face seemed to harden and set in dissatisfaction.

Tzirel noted her husband's evident discontent and could

contain herself no longer. Was this letter not a definite reason for rejoicing? Even the children, naive as they are, realized the good fortune that the letter brought them. Why was he, Tuvya, the only one to dismiss their doubled income with a shrug of his shoulders? It was too much for Tzirel to comprehend. She lashed into her husband, demanding that instead of moping and drooping, he unburden his troubled heart to her.

His answer was brief and decisive. "I have resolved to break off this partnership with Yona Tabak."

"What?" Tzirel cried out in utter disbelief. "What has happened all of a sudden?"

"I can't . . ." faltered Reb Tuvya. "I find no satisfaction in the arrangement. Rav Shmuel will surely accept me in the yeshiva and I will support myself like all the other scholars. . ."

"Have you discussed this yet with the Rav?" Tzirel asked. "Did he tell you to do this? Or have you decided without consulting him? It is not right, you know, since he is the one who originally drew up the contract."

Obstacles

REB TUVYA opened his mouth to answer his wife, but was interrupted by a sudden intruder. Reb Yaakov Edelman, who served as Rav Shmuel's messenger, hurried into the house. "The Rav is waiting for you!" he announced.

What urgent matter requires me to appear before the Rav? Reb Tuvya wondered as he rapidly followed Reb Yaakov.

Actually, the matter did not concern Reb Tuvya at all. It concerned Itcha Pinsker, the water-carrier of the Churva courtyard. Itcha had dared defy the strict prohibition of the Torah-leaders in the Old City; he had transferred his five year-old Yisraelke from the Talmud Torah *cheider* to Dr. Hertzberg's secular school.

Itcha was summoned to stand in judgment before Rav Shmuel Salant, Rav of Jerusalem, but his shame made him send his wife — who was really responsible for the transgression — in his stead. She came — for who dared defy Rav Shmuel — and stood dejectedly in a corner of the room, awaiting her judgment. Rav Shmuel sat at his table and asked for an explanation. It was too much for 'he poor woman. Overcome suddenly by all her burdens,
` very burdens that had made her take such a drastic step to begin with, the water-carrier's wife broke down in front of Rav Shmuel. The explanations, punctuated by sobs and tears, burst forth from her lips.

"My house is bare. We haven't even a crumb to feed

the poor little ones, much less to pay their tuition! Starved, ragged, and cold, their sad, pale faces stare at me.... I was at the end of my rope when a neighbor suggested that I transfer my Yisraelke to the school. There, she promised, I wouldn't have to worry about tuition; the boy would get three meals daily and even clothes to wear. I really had no choice. So I followed her advice."

The words tumbled from her mouth in a torrent of emotion and self-justification. But Rav Shmuel stopped her short in the middle and spoke sternly, "Enough! You must go immediately and remove the boy from that school. I command it. When you have done that you may return here and I will listen to whatever else you have to say." Not daring to argue, she bowed her head and left the house to do as she had been bidden.

It was at this point that the Rav called his messenger, Reb Yaakov Edelman, to fetch Reb Tuvya immediately. A devoted and energetic servant of the Rav's, Reb Yaakov soon had his mission accomplished and Reb Tuvya stood at the Rav's door.

Rav Shmuel bade his visitor enter. He described the scene that had just taken place with a brief explanatory background. "And so you see," he came to the point, "if the boy Yisraelke is not removed from his environment he will be lost to Yiddishkeit. Without a shadow of doubt he must be wrenched away from Dr. Hertzberg's noxious establishment, but he must just as surely be taken away from his home, for his parents have dealt with him capriciously.

"The parents are weak-willed people, concerned only with their daily bread. Their feeble character could even lead them to deliver their children to the missions, God forbid. Another home must be found for the boy, a home that will care for his spiritual wants as well as for his physical needs. My advice is, therefore, that you, Reb Tuvya, take the boy into your home. Treat him as you do your own children, let him eat at your table, study with your sons. Care for him as if he were your own flesh and blood. Watch over him, guard him until he grows into an independent adult who can be relied on to know right from wrong. You have been blessed with a bountiful income and freedom from financial burdens. It is therefore your blessing, your merit, and and your obligation to save this soul from spiritual destruction."

Rav Shmuel waited for Reb Tuvya's reaction, but the latter did not reply. A strained stillness reigned in the room. Did Reb Tuvya fear retribution from the child's parents?

Not Reb Tuvya. He was a fearless man and had been known for his courage back in Minsk, courage for the sake of Torah and its sacred *mitzvoth*. Reb Tuvya was not a man to shirk responsibility either, so that could not be the reason for his silence.

Reb Tuvya's conscience smote him from a different direction altogether. He had just professed the desire to cut off his source of income by breaking his ties with Reb Yona Tabak. Under such circumstances, how could he possibly take a strange boy into his home? He had prepared to rejoice in his new lot of poverty, to be on an equal footing with his friends, chiefly Reb Simcha. Did Rav Shmuel's plan come now to foil his own intentions? Reb Tuvya stood in a quandary, not knowing what to say or what to think. Should he reveal his innermost thoughts or should he find some way out without explaining his reasons? Meanwhile Rav Shmuel was looking at him both expectantly and benignly, waiting for an answer.

"I must ask my wife first," Reb Tuvya finally managed to say. "She is, after all, the one who must make such a major decision, for the burden will fall mainly upon her shoulders."

"Nu, nu," agreed Rav Shmuel with a fatherly nod of his head.

Reb Tuvya unfolded the story to his wife, but before he had even finished outlining the last part, the one that concerned them personally, Tzirel interrupted excitedly, "Of course I agree, and wholeheartedly, too. What an opportunity to do good! How fortunate we are that such a mitzva has come our way!" she exclaimed, her whole being beaming brightly. "Go quickly and tell the Rav that we are both happy and proud to accept with all our hearts. Hurry," she almost pushed him out of the door, "someone else may beat us to it and snatch our mitzva away from under us. Oh, how happy I am. We will take this boy into our home and into our hearts. We will educate him in the true ways of our Torah and enrich him with an eternal heritage. Such a mitzva does not knock at one's door every day. Go! Quickly!"

And as he was leaving she called after him, "And don't forget to thank the Rav for having us in mind for this wonderful mitzva."

Tzirel's words, her whole attitude, had a powerful effect upon Reb Tuvya, potent enough to make him reconsider his earlier decision to break his ties with Reb Yona Tabak. He looked at his spiritual world with different eyes now, no longer envious eyes that saw his friends surpassing him in piety and scholarship. He now saw his world as two — one extra world gained by taking an unfortunate young soul under his wing and transforming it into a worthy vessel. It was with considerably less reluctance that Reb Tuvya hurried back to grasp the mitzva while it was still being offered to him.

"And *you?*" Rav Shmuel asked perceptively in reply to

Reb Tuvya's announcement of his wife's willingness to take the boy into his home, "What do *you* say to my proposition? Do you agree, too?" This direct question hit home. Reb Tuvya could not prevaricate; he could hide nothing from his teacher and mentor. The words jumped out of his mouth as if alive. All the pent-up emotion, the heartache, and the gnawing doubts found expression as Reb Tuvya described his deep desire to study Torah under conditions of poverty as his peers did.

Rav Shmuel let the man rid his system of its haunting doubts. Reb Tuvya spoke at length, and the old Rav gave him his full attention. When he had finished speaking, Reb Tuvya stood silently, begging with his eyes that the Rav make the difficult decision for him. Rav Shmuel did not answer at first. Then the old Rav arose and painfully made his way to the bookcase, from which he removed an ancient manuscript written by a scholar who had lived over four hundred years before. Still not breaking the emotion-packed silence, Rav Shmuel turned to the introduction and handed the manuscript to Reb Tuvya, bidding him to read it.

Reb Tuvya took the faded, frail scroll and read aloud, The man whom God has blessed with wealth and property should not make light of his wealth and should not hasten to dispose of it, for not every fortune tends to corrupt its owner. The wise man, whose eyes are in the right place, will use his wealth to good advantage for purposes that bring satisfaction to his Maker. As we have seen in the past, pious men who were blessed with wealth and property did not enjoy their own bounty even to the extent of their little finger, as our Sages testify for Rabbeinu haKadosh. Rabbi Yehuda haNassi lifted his ten fingers up before him, as he was about to die, to bear witness that he had not enjoyed this world for its own sake, in any measure whatsoever, despite his tremendous wealth. One can cause the Holy One, blessed be He, no greater pleasure than by utilizing one's fortune for lofty purposes such as saving lives, working for the public good, and so on, and anyone who disposes of his wealth thus, is certain of a goodly portion in the world-to-come.

Before Reb Tuvya finished reading these few lines he had grasped the Rav's message. It was quite apparent that all the roads to his personal desire of Torah-through-poverty were blocked. His future had been laid out, and all other gates to the world-to-come were barred to him. Reb Tuvya's dream was shattered once and for all.

Rav Shmuel had willed differently than Reb Tuvya would have wished for himself. There was no way out. With a reluctant sigh of resignation, he rerolled the dusty manuscript and handed it back to Rav Shmuel. He did not say a word, but twin tears glistened in the corners of his eyes.

Boy Missing

REB TUVYA returned home to await the arrival of the new addition to his family. He and Tzirel stood by the window expectantly until they finally saw Reb Leib Cheifetz approaching, leading a little boy by the hand. They both rushed out to greet the little stranger and to make him feel at home.

The boy entered their home and their hearts. Reb Tuvya and his wife shared their good fortune. Tzirel fed and clothed the boy, clucking over him like a mother hen, while Reb Tuvya looked after his education. They cared for him with dedicated zeal and holy fire, treating him like a treasure — a treasured mitzva that had been sent their way. Little Yisraelke, showered with fatherly and motherly love, felt like one of the family — if anything, like a privileged member of the family. The water-carrier's son lived a happy and sheltered life with the Feldshers.

On the morning following his arrival, the little boy was taken to *cheider* to study under the tutelage of Reb Hirsh Denenburg, an expert *melamed* and Godfearing man. Reb Tuvya would visit the *cheider* every day to inquire after the boy's progress. In contrast to this devotion, Yisraelke's parents showed no concern for his welfare and their strange indifference struck everyone as odd.

These good days in the Feldsher household did not last long. That Purim after the reading of the *megilla,* Yisraelke left Reb Tuvya's home in disguise. He was carrying a silver tray stacked high with delicacies to be delivered to

Students of the Talmud Torah and Yeshiva Etz Chayim

A Yerushalmi child

Rav Shneyur Zalman of Lublin as a *mishlo'ach manoth* gift. And that was the last seen of the boy.

In vain did Reb Tuvya and his wife await Yisraelke's return. Two hours passed and he did not come back. "Maybe he stayed in the Rav's house," Tzirel suggested "It must be teeming with chassidim drinking and making merry. The boy might have remained there to soak up the Purim atmosphere." But as more time went by and he still did not appear, her doubts took the upper hand. "Maybe he lost his way," she admitted.

"What do you mean 'lost his way'?" Reb Tuvya answered. "He accompanies me there every Shaboss. How could he have suddenly lost his way?"

It was past *mincha* time. The sun was beginning to set and Jews all over Jerusalem were rejoicing in the festive meal, except for Reb Tuvya and his household. There the air was tense. The couple had decided that a search was necessary. Reb Tuvya's first stop was at the home of the Lubliner Rav, but neither the Rav nor anyone in his house had seen the boy. Of that they were certain.

It wasn't long before the whole city was seething with the news. Night had begun to fall; scattered groups of stars twinkled above the narrow streets. Small groups of holiday revelers and happy drunkards still reeled and rollicked in the streets, unwilling to relinquish their hold upon this once-a-year day of gaiety and carefree joy. But the rest of the inhabitants forgot their holiday spirits in their concern for the boy. Everyone had a different conjecture, a bit of advice, a word of sympathy. But no one had any clue as to what had actually become of the boy, who seemed to have disappeared into the thick Purim air.

No amount of sympathy could ease the pain that Reb Tuvya and his wife felt. No reproach, had it been uttered, could have been as biting as their self-reproach at having

A rebbe and his cheider of those days

sent Yisraelke out alone. Their intention, to initiate the boy in the independent performance of mitzvoth, had been pure. The Jerusalem streets had throbbed with little children and big trays. Purim was verily their day of free-for-all. No, the Feldshers could not be reproached for any laxity in love or vigil for their charge. But the blows their own conscience dealt them made their burden unbearable. The members of the Feldsher household combed the streets and examined the alleyways, looking high and low in likely and unlikely places. They were joined in their fruit-less search by groups of laborers, yeshiva scholars and tradesmen. The town crier spread the news in all the corners of the city, enlisting the aid of all able-bodied men to help in the search and to gather information about the lost boy and where he was last seen. Tension grew in the city, and surprise was expressed at the indifference of the real parents of the boy, the water-carrier and his wife, and their refusal to join in the search. Everyone looked askance at people who so unnaturally removed themselves from a matter which had become, in the short span of an hour, of major public concern. Itcha was seen dragging his pails of water as usual. His wife continued at her washtub, scrubbing away without any hint of new cares. And when questioned about the boy they both shrugged their shoulders noncommitally. It was their very unconcern that directed a whole new train of theories regarding what had befallen Yisraelke.

The Turkish police force was called into the picture. Patrolmen and plainclothesmen scoured the countryside, refusing, however, to consider the possibility that the boy might be within the Old City limits.

Having done all that was humanly possible, Reb Tuvya and his wife returned home to digest the bitter pill of defeat and despair.

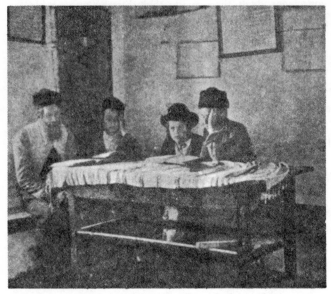

A rebbe and his cheider of those days

Kidnaper Found

JERUSALEM of old was blessed with a wealth of 'types,' or one-of-a-kind people, individualists. No less a type was Isaac Breksler — handyman, street-cleaner, gossipmonger.

Skinny as a broomstick, tall, bald, his lower face covered by a mere excuse of a beard, thick-lipped, crosseyed but smiling, Isaac's appearance was as simple as his personality. Nor did this singular appearance stop at his face. The reddish silk turban he wound about his head summer and winter in the manner of the Sefaradim, and the silk caftan which flapped around his ankles, completed the exterior picture of a one-of-a-kind character, half-Sefaradi and half-Ashkenazi, as he was indeed by birth.

Isaac's greatest pleasure was to gab. His strange but entertaining stories, though they changed continually, were familiar to all. There was no event, either public or private, about which Isaac did not know, did not tell, and did not express his personal comments. He knew of all *shidduchim* before the *chathan* and *kalla* themselves did, knew of clandestine meetings before they even took place, of events in royal courtyards and in peasant hovels. His vast knowledge encompassed world politics. Isaac was privy to the latest decrees that the Russian Czar was planning; he instinctively 'knew' where, anywhere on the face of the globe, war was to break out, and which fleet would defeat what army. If you asked for the information, he gave it. If you didn't, he told it to you anyway.

There was, however, another side to the marketplace-cleaner savant of Jerusalem, for Isaac had many fans, scores of people who vouched for the gold interior which lay beneath the ludicrous surface. Isaac, they averred, never went to work without first going to immerse himself in the *mikveh*, praying at the early pre-sunrise *vathikin minyan* and then reviewing the daily *Chok LeYisrael* portion. Isaac had a big heart and was ready to forgive anyone for anything, to forego any personal pleasure. But his *mikveh* bath, his *vathikin minyan* and his *Chok* were inviolate. He guarded these daily practices tenaciously. Others would tell about his steady practice of tithing his meager salary each day among the poor — the poorer, that is — at the Kothel haMa'aravi. And the stories about him did not stop there either.

One can easily imagine that the furor raised over the lost child kept Isaac very busy. Wherever a group of Jews gathered to discuss the matter, Isaac was present, as if he had miraculously sprung from the ground under their feet. And when Isaac appeared at any gathering he immediately became the center of attention. Regardless of whether they actually believed him or not, everyone listened to Isaac. He had a way with words, a style of storytelling that magnetized and charmed his audience, despite a stutter that would break out now and then in the course of his fascinating tales. Rather than mar the effect, it enhanced his delivery, giving it a certain charm.

People of purpose rarely indulged in the entertainment that Isaac provided at streetcorners or in his stage-setting of the marketplace. But this Purim was an exception. Even Reb Simcha stopped to hear what Isaac had to say about the missing child.

"And I t-tell you," Isaac began, stuttering with an exaggerated sense of self-importance at having in his audience such an important person as Reb Simcha Polnoa, "that the b-boy you are all searching for is in the home of Dr. Hertzberg. He k-kidnaped him for his cursed school."

"And how do you know this bit of information?" Reb Simcha asked sharply.

"Nu, nu, who doesn't know that?"

"Even so. . ." Reb Simcha tried to lead him on to reveal any further information he might know or guess at.

"Ha, Ha, Ha!" Isaac guffawed. "What do you m-mean, 'How does Isaac know'?" As if Dr. Hertzberg didn't spend many a night by Itcha the water-carrier."

Why had Dr. Hertzberg visited the water-carrier in the middle of the night? Nobody knew. It surely couldn't be that he had developed a sudden burning thirst for water in the middle of the night. Was it the company he enjoyed there? The atmosphere? The surroundings of that damp cellar apartment?

Having received no comments on his theory, Isaac felt it necessary to repeat his point. "I still say, Reb Simcha, that that *apikoress* was the one who snatched the child."

There was no reaction, no sign of agreement. Isaac shook his head dolefully and intoned, "Oy! Oy! You'll see, you'll say yet that Isaac was right," and he disappeared to find himself a more receptive audience elsewhere.

Unknown to Isaac, however, his words did indeed have a profound effect on Reb Simcha. He sped to Reb Tuvya.

"Listen, my good friend. My heart tells me that the child has vanished into Dr. Hertzberg's home. I suggest we go there immediately and search for him before it is too late."

"Who would dare enter Dr. Hertzberg's house?" Reb Tuvya asked, hope and fear alternating on his face. "He is an Austrian citizen, you know. The Austrian ambassador is very protective toward Austrian citizens in this country, especially since his government is on excellent terms with the Turkish rulers. He would probably not suffer anyone to touch a hair of one of his countrymen, besides which he and Dr. Hertzberg are personally very close friends and have been for a long time. How do you propose to begin to go about it?"

Reb Simcha was at a loss to answer, but not for long. The optimist in him had come up with an idea. "Let us go to Rav Chayim Sonnenfeld. In his wisdom he will devise a plan for us," Reb Simcha suggested hopefully.

Reb Tuvya let his friend take the lead and they went forth. As they neared the Churva synagogue they became aware of a huge crowd. Confusion reigned and loud voices drowned one another out. Curious to know the cause of the commotion, they approached and were singled out by none other than Isaac Breksler, who was overjoyed at the opportunity of capturing an interested and important audience. Unfortunaely for Isaac, his stutter overpowered him and the two good friends could not make any sense of his words. They drew closer to the center of the circle and could hear Reb Leib Cheifetz hurling threats and abuses at Dr. Hertzberg, who was just passing by.

"You are wrecking the holy city of Jerusalem. You are destroying it. Is that why you came here? To establish your cursed school which leads Jewish children to apostasy? What do you have against the untainted souls of Jewish children who have not sinned, that you amputate their souls from their rightful eternal heritage?"

A crowd had immediately formed when Reb Leib began to shout. It surrounded the accuser and the accused, forming a tight ring around the two and preventing Dr. Hertzberg from slipping away. The doctor's friends came to the rescue by summoning the Turkish police to disperse the crowd. When the police demanded to know who had started the street scene, Dr. Hertzberg's friends pointed to Reb Leib, and the man was apprehended on the spot.

Reb Tuvya and Reb Simcha, witnesses to the whole scene, now forgot all about their original intention of visiting Rav Chayim Sonnenfeld. They retraced their steps and went to Rav Shmuel Salant to bear the sad news of Reb Leib's imprisonment and to beg him to intervene. Rav Shmuel instantly penned a short, caustic letter to the Chief of Police, and taking this bit of ammunition, the two sped to the Kishla jail in the Armenian quarter of the Old City. To their disappointment, the Chief of Police was not there, but they resolved not to budge from the spot until they had succeeded in releasing the unfortunate Reb Leib.

It was a long wait, but they had each other and all the Torah they knew by heart. They reviewed the *Gemara* they had been studying together, discussing its questions and answers at length. Then they went on to review some *Mishnayoth* and culminated with the recital of *Tehilim*, choosing from the *alef-beith* verses of Psalm 119 the verses that began with the letters of Reb Leib's name, hoping that their prayers for the good man's speedy release would be heard and answered.

The Chief of Police finally appeared. They handed him the letter from Rav Shmuel and sat down to wait while he entered a private office. After about another half hour, he emerged to tell them that their man was free to go.

It was only minutes before they were reunited with their good acquaintance. "You are fortunate to have been jailed for Torah," they exclaimed joyfully, repeating the famous words Papus ben Yehuda had said to Rabbi Akiva, as they vigorously shook his hand. Reb Leib beamed happily.

67

On their way back to the Jewish quarter, Reb Leib told his two companions what had actually happened:

"Reb Meshulam the pharmacist, one of Jerusalem's precious Jews, neighbor of Dr. Hertzberg, saw the boy with his *peyoth* shorn off, walking around in Dr. Hertzberg's home. When he told me that, I felt an uncontrollable zealous fire rage inside me. That a man who professes to be an educated and enlightened person should stoop to such gangster tactics as kidnaping! Then when I saw the man, I could not contain myself."

Reb Leib could barely contain himself in recalling the incident. He begged his friends to join him in charging into Dr. Hertzberg's home then and there to demand the boy back. "Let us at least organize a group of yeshiva people who can help us by the strength of their numbers," he suggested when they seemed to reject his enthusiastic plans.

They couldn't very well do that, they told the heated Reb Leib. They reminded him that Dr. Hertzberg was an Austrian citizen and explained what significance this had. If they attempted to right the matter through force, it would put Dr. Hertzberg in a more favorable light and their cause would only suffer. "Our wisest step at this point would be to go to Rav Chayim Sonnenfeld. He will handle the matter without being intimidated by any authority, wisely as well as fearlessly."

This suggestion pleased Reb Leib. And so, the twosome turned threesome found themselves back where they had started many hours earlier that day.

At the Kothel haMaaravi

IT WAS ALMOST MIDNIGHT and the clear Jerusalem
skies were seeded with shining stars. The Batey Machseh
neighborhood, its red shingled rooftops reflecting the sil-
very moon, slept peacefully under those friendly skies. All
was still with the exception of one sound that broke the
unfathomable stillness for any ears that chanced to hear
it. It was the low wailing of Reb Hirsh Michel Heller's
tikkun chatzoth, the midnight bewailing of the destroyed
batey hamikdash.

The threesome felt their way cautiously through the dark
streets and up the steps of the narrow Old City alleys.
With some difficulty they finally arrived at Rav Chayim
Sonnenfeld's dwelling, a house hewn out of the very
mountain. Reb Leib knocked at the door several times.
No answer. Where could Reb Chayim be at such an
unearthly hour, the three men wondered. As if in answer
to their unspoken question, a head popped out of a
nearby window and informed them that the *tzaddik* had
just left for the Kothel. The three headed toward the
Kothel.

The small courtyard of the Kothel was deserted. It
loomed like an ancient, fearful fortress in the pale light of
the dead of night. The nine gigantic boulders that King
David had prepared for the foundation of God's chosen
home seemed to whisper mysteriously to one another.
During the day, the courtyard was filled with Jews from

all walks of life, each bearing his personal burden, each pouring out his bitter heart to the listening stones and obtaining relief. At *mincha* and *maariv* time, dozens of Jews from the yeshivos in the Old City would gather here to pray together and then drift off into corners to complete their individual obligations for the day, a few chapters of *Tehilim* here, some requests from the *Techina* there. And then, prayer-sated, they would drift off, leaving the Kothel to wail alone in the night and whisper back the sad tales it had heard during the day. The last to leave would be the *shamash*, who, after gathering the *siddurim* and *Tehilims* together and locking them up in a tiny closet, would lovingly kiss the familiar stones and respectfully depart.

When the area was deserted and the night closed in on one, Rav Chayim Sonnenfeld would go down to the Kothel to commune with himself, with the stones, with his Creator. Only then could he truly open his heart to release the pent-up love and concern he felt for his suffering brothers. Only then, in the ringing stillness, as he stared at the sole remnant of the *beith ha-mikdash* area, could he express the loss he felt for the *beith ha-mikdash*. Huddled in a corner, he would stand motionless and pray soundlessly to the Divine Presence that had deserted its home and had gone into exile. Like a son beseeching his father would he open up the wells of his heart and pray, and, as he prayer, an aura of purity and sanctity descended upon him and illuminated his lonely figure.

Not daring to disturb the *tzaddik* at his prayers, the three men stood off to the side and waited respectfully for him to finish. One hour, two hours passed and Reb Tuvya, Reb Simcha, and Reb Leib felt the weariness of their trying day eating into their flesh and bones.

At first they had thought that Rav Chayim had come to recite the *tikkun chatzoth* but as hour after hour passed they realized that they had been mistaken. Nevertheless they waited on wearily, patiently, reverently. When their fatigue threatened to overcome their last resources of energy, they sat down on the cold, dew-moistened stone floor and continued to wait in silence. What was the secret of the *tzaddik's* interminable nighttime prayers? No one dared wonder aloud. Rav Chayim's wife would often tell how her husband kept this nightly appointment at the Kothel only to return for the early *vathikin* prayers. She knew full well that he went there to pour out his heart in prayer, but what the purpose of that prayer was, anyone could conjecture as well as she.

With the coming of the rosy dawn light the stars twinkled and flickered out one by one, departing to make way for the magnificent ruler of the day, the sun. It was just about to announce its arrival with a burst of majesty when Rav Chayim, having finished his prayers, turned to leave his corner and suddenly came upon the three men huddled on the stone floor, half-dozing, half-praying. They got up in quick confusion and proceeded to accompany the *tzaddik* homeward, narrating the story of Yisraelka, the water-carrier's son, from its sad beginning to its sad stalemate. Reb Leib described how he came to know that the boy was indeed in Dr. Hertzberg's house.

"We must do something immediately, before the boy is so poisoned as to refuse to return, at which point he will be entirely lost to us," he cried out impatiently.

Rav Chayim listened carefully, asking for all the details of the story. Reb Tuvya elaborated on Dr. Hertzberg's Austrian citizenship and its many ramifications. They finished their story just as they brought Rav Chayim to the gate that led to his *Batey Machseh* home.

He surely wishes to daven vathikin prayers now, they thought, *and we must not disturb him further.* And so, signaling to one another, they left him standing there, confident that Rav Chayim would not let the day go by without doing something for their cause. It was not important what or how. They trusted his wisdom, his tirelessness, and his fearlessness. Rav Chayim's zealous sense of responsibility would not allow him to neglect so vital a matter as saving the soul of a Jewish boy. As the threesome dissolved, each man to go his own way, their hearts whispered to them that their mission was in the surest hands and on the threshold of victory.

At the Ambassador's

NO SOONER HAD the three men disappeared around the bend than Rav Chayim retraced his steps. Completely ablaze with the conviction of Torah that saving a life takes precedence over any other mitzva, he headed toward the Austrian Embassy which sprawled just beyond the Damascus Gate.

Meanwhile, in the Batey Machseh synagogue, situated in Rav Chayim's own attic, the worshippers had been waiting for Rav Chayim to appear and signal the begining of the *vathikin* service, as he had done every day for years. They had waited half an hour already and only fifteen minutes remained until sunrise. Neither heat nor cold, weakness nor illness ever deterred Rav Chayim from his punctual attendance at the *vathikin minyan*. The assembled worshipers guessed that something unusual was afoot today, something important enough to make Rav Chayim break with his tradition of many years. And so they decided to start without him. Unknown to them, at the moment the *chazan* was reciting *"V'al ha-tzaddikim,"* their own *tzaddik* was already standing by the iron gate that barred the entry to the Austrian ambassador's mansion.

The Turkish gendarmes who guarded the structure barely had an opportunity to explain to Rav Chayim how impossible was his request to gain entry — at that hour and without a written request and an appointment made a day earlier — when who should descend the marble

73

staircase but His Excellency the Ambassador himself. Dressed in his morning robe, his thick, flourishing moustache not yet brushed and waxed, the old man approached the iron gates and ushered in his visitor with astonishing warmth. The guards followed the pair with open-mouthed amazement as the ambassador took his guest's arm and graciously led him into a drawing room, even pulling out a chair for the Jewish rabbi and begging him to sit down.

There was good reason for this wave of astonishment which rolled over the whole courtyard, swelling to tidal proportions as servants and lower members of the ambassador's household also beheld these strange phenomena. Their master was not in the habit of rising so early. His gruff pompousness was rarely broken by a smile or any hint of a kind word. The ambassador never saw someone without a previous appointment. How, then, had this Jewish rabbi broken through all these barriers without a word?

The members of Rav Chayim's household, however, would not have reacted with such amazement. The ambassador's high esteem for Rav Chayim dated back two years to an incident which had revealed to the gentile a small measure of Rav Chayim's greatness. Ever since then, he had accorded the rabbi tremendous respect.

★

The incident had concerned a Jewish Hungarian couple in Grossvardein. While the husband had spent his time in Torah study, the wife had managed a flourishing business that had expanded to many branches in different cities and made wealthy people of them both. The only thing that marred their happiness was their childlessness.

One day the wife brought the sum of four hundred gulden, a small fortune in those days, to her local Rav. "I want to relay this money as a donation to some great rabbi so that he may pray that I bear children," she instructed.

The Rav considered the huge sum before him and suggested, "If you truly want the money to go to proper hands, send it to Rav Chayim Sonnenfeld to Jerusalem. He will surely be able to help you."

The woman agreed heartily and the money was dispatched that very day. It was not sent directly, however, since the diplomatic relations between the Turkish and Austrian governments were strained, and a major portion of the mail never reached its destination. Instead it was sent to the Austrian ambassador in Palestine to be forwarded to Rav Chayim.

When the Austrian ambassador in Jerusalem received this huge sum of money, he was curious to meet its intended recipient, whom he knew to be a poor Jew living within the Old City walls. The curious ambassador read the letter accompanying the money.

Two weeks passed, and the husband learned of his wife's generous gift to the unknown-to-him rabbi in Jerusalem. When the husband upbraided the local Rav for having accepted such a huge sum without consulting him, the Rav justified his action by arguing that he had been certain that the woman had acted with her husband's knowledge and approval. The husband was somewhat calmed but he insisted that the Rav write to Rav Cha'yim and demand the money back, explaining that it had been sent by mistake.

The Rav was extremely reluctant to comply. "Let me rather repay the sum from my own pocket in monthly installments," he begged. The husband would not hear of it.

While they stood there stalemated, the postman knocked, bringing a letter from Jerusalem. It was from Rav

Yoseif Chayim Sonnenfeld and it contained the four
hundred gulden together with a letter in which he explained
why he was returning the money. The Rav read it aloud,

> I received your letter in which you inform me that
> the woman brought the money herself. Since I fear
> that she may have taken this money without her
> husband's consent, I am returning the entire sum
> to you, begging you respectfully to return it to its
> rightful owner. May I add that this will have no
> effect upon my prayers that the woman be blessed
> with a child. God's deliverance comes as speedily
> as an eyeblink.

The husband and wife stood there dumfounded. Only
their eyes, overflowing with tears, expressed their emotions.
Such sensitivity as Rav Chayim had displayed, such
nobility and strength of character, was beyond their
imagination. In his new-found deep respect, the husband
immediately asked the Rav to send the money back
to Jerusalem with a note expressing his desire that Rav
Chayim keep the money. "It will be a tremendous merit
for my money to go to such a *tzaddik*," he said fervently.

The Austrian ambassador had been following the
developments with growing interest and a deepening respect
for Rav Chayim. The story made an indelible impression
upon him, and he determined to meet this unusual man
face to face. One night he went alone to Batey Machseh
and there, in the strange little apartment hewn out of
mountain rock, the two men sat talking for hours on end
and formed a lasting friendship. The more the Austrian
spoke to the rabbi, the more he came to revere him for
his wisdom and exceptional character.

★

It was no wonder, then, that he had rushed forward to
personally greet Rav Chayim even at this early hour.

Now, seated in a comfortable leather chair in the ambassador's drawing room, Rav Chayim spoke briefly and to the point,

"The purpose of my visit is to present the plea of the thousands of Godfearing Jews here that Your Excellency demand in unequivocal terms that Dr. Hertzberg return the boy immediately."

"What do you mean?" asked the ambassador in complete surprise.

Rav Chayim explained, "About two weeks ago, a boy disappeared from the Jewish quarter. The son of poor people, he had recently been adopted by another family headed by a Jew named Tuvya. A widespread search was conducted by the adoptive family, by friends, and even by the Turkish authorities, but it proved fruitless. All hope was practically abandoned until it was learned that the boy had been kidnaped by Dr. Hertzberg's men in order to enroll him in the secular school and tear him away from his traditional heritage, the religious education he had been receiving under the supervision of his adopted father."

"What? A secular education under Dr. Hertzberg! He is a religious Jew! Upon my occasional visits to his house, he always tells me about his many plans in the educational field. He believes, for example, that the religious education in Jerusalem is deficient, that it is below standard. He intends to improve it and to infuse it with a modern spirit which will fit the times by incorporating European ideas in education."

The ambassador even had a story to back his words. He told it triumphantly. "About a month ago I was invited by Dr. Hertzberg to visit his school. I was busy all through the day and only found a free minute toward evening. When I approached the schoolyard a marvelous scene met my eyes. The children were all lined up under the starry sky with prayerbooks in their hands, reciting something by the light of the moon. He later explained that they were blessing the new moon, a Jewish ceremony that they repeated each month.

"When the children finished their prayer," the ambassador continued enthusiastically, "Dr. Hertzberg took me on a tour of the institution. In the dining room I saw boys washing their hands before eating and reciting grace after the meal. As I learned upon a different occasion, these are practices common only to observant Jews. How can you then say that this institution is a secular one?" he concluded triumphantly with the air of one who has had the very last word.

Rav Chayim answered calmly, "Your Excellency no doubt remembers the imprisonment of Dr. Helmar, the personal friend of the Austrian Minister of Defense who served during the French-Austrian War in the past century." The ambassador nodded and Rav Chayim continued, "It was common knowledge that Dr. Helmar was the top adviser and personal confidant to the minister. All of the minister's programs and plans passed through his hands. In addition he was appointed as tutor to the minister's children as a result of the high esteem and great regard which the minister had for him. But in one short evening, Helmar's whole cart was overturned. The minister was taking a turn in his garden accompanied by his firstborn. Suddenly out of the blue, the boy burst into a French march tune. The Austrian minister's nationalistic pride was wounded and he demanded to know where his son had picked up the enemy song. The boy naively answered that his tutor had taught it to him among many other songs in his French culture lessons, to which they devoted many hours. The minister's face grew suffused with rage. He culminated his pleasure walk and returned to the house immediately. There he summoned the culprit tutor and confronted him with the information he had just learned. 'At the very time that the cream of Austrian youth is dying in battle, at the time our valiant soldiers are soaking our earth with their blood in a bitter struggle against the enemy for the glory of the Fatherland — you dare inculcate my son with enemy culture?! You are guilty of treason in the very face of battle!'

"As a man guilty of treason," Rav Chayim continued, "he was court-martialed before a military tribunal and sentenced to life imprisonment."

Rav Chayim lost his calm manner. He arose from the easy chair he had been occupying and exclaimed vehemently, "Dr. Hertzberg also schemes to implant into the untutored hearts of our tender children a foreign culture, the very treacherous culture that was responsible for the burning of tens of thousands of Jewish children, the Western European culture that extirpated them from their life-giving roots, annihilating them spiritually and physically.

"We Jews," Rav Chayim went on to explain in calmer tones, "came to this holy land with only one purpose in mind: to serve God and educate the next generation in our traditional heritage which we received from our holy forefathers. And behold, schemers like Dr. Hertzberg appear on the scene and threaten to graft foreign branches onto the Jewish vine. They aim to poison untainted souls whose purity we guard like the apples of our eyes."

Rav Chayim Sonnenfeld's forceful words gave the ambassador an insight into the enigma of the lives and aims of Jerusalem Jewry. The gentile ambassador was deeply moved. He arose and grasped Rav Chayim's hand fervently, "My honored friend, you may rest assured. I give you my word of honor that within six hours the boy will be returned."

*Banner of greeting for Kaiser Wilhelm II on his visit
to Jerusalem*

Having accomplished his purpose, Rav Chayim felt that there was no further cause for him to extend the conversation. He thanked his host sincerely, and after the ambassador had accorded him the final honor of accompanying his respected guest until the very gate. he took his leave.

The Return

HAVING MISSED his *vathikin minyan,* Rav Chayim stopped
off to daven in the Churva *shul* and joined one of the
tradesmen's *minyanim.* After the davening he offered a
special prayer to the Provident God Who had made his
mission of saving a Jewish soul a successful one and
Who had tempered the gentile ambassador's heart to listen
to his words and to be influenced by them. Rav Chayim
then left the *shul* and headed homeward. In all of the city
there was not a soul who knew of his visit to the awesome
and autocratic Austrian ambassador and of its successful
outcome. The *tzaddik* simply attached no importance to his
own part in the story. He had merely done his duty; he
had fulfilled a necessary function at the request of three
Jerusalem citizens, to save a Jewish child from spiritual perdition. Nothing more. Was one hour invested in
saving a Jewish life such a great sacrifice?

However, the same Providence that had helped him find
favor in the eyes of the gentile ambassador also intended
Rav Chayim's greatness to be revealed. One of the
ambassador's Jewish clerks heard the ambassador repeat
the story to his acquaintances, and he in turn caused the
incident to become the *cause célèbre* of the day on the lips
of all Jerusalem's inhabitants.

Morning was just turning into afternoon when Rav
Chayim returned home to find an important caller awaiting him. One of the ambassador's bodyguards stood hold-

ing a little boy by the hand. He bowed deeply when he saw the *tzaddik*, and introduced himself, explained that the ambassador had sent him to deliver the water-carrier's kidnaped boy. Word of the impressive gentile visitor spread on wings and curious neighbors congregated immediately outside Rav Chayim's house, eager to squeeze the story out of the guard. He willingly obliged, flattered by the huge audience that had gathered to hear him.

"Early this morning," he explained with relish, "I was sent by the ambassador to deliver a note to Dr. Hertzberg. I was ordered to reinforce it by adding verbally that if he did not comply with haste, he would suffer harsh consequences. I hurried to fulfill my orders. When Dr. Hertzberg read the note, he scowled angrily but entered a nearby house to fetch the boy who had just awoken. Muttering some German curses under his breath, he handed him over to me.

"At first the boy refused to accompany me, dressed up as I was in my colorful official guard's uniform, but Dr. Hertzberg himself coaxed the lad to go with the 'Uncle'."

His moment of glory over, the guard left the child in welcome hands and returned whence he had come. Yisraelka was promptly returned to his foster parents, Reb Tuvya and his wife Tzirel, who gathered him lovingly and with added fervor into their hearts and home, where he remained without further complications for the remainder of his childhood.

Jerusalem veterans add a postscript to the story. They relate that the two weeks that Yisraelke spent in Dr. Hertzberg's secular institution affected him adversely, causing him to lose his taste for Torah-study; the boy's original pure tendencies had been tainted. Reb Tuvya broached the problem of the boy's education to Rav

Yosef Chayim Sonnenfeld, feeling that since he had already taken a personal interest in the matter he would certainly want to see it through to a happy conclusion. Rav Chayim suggested that the boy be apprenticed to Reb Nissan Shuster, the shoemaker-*tzaddik* Reb Tuvya had met in his first week in Jerusalem. How the shoemaker succeeded in capturing Yisraelke's interest and his heart, no one really knows. In any case, the boy grew close to his tutor. Though he only absorbed a small measure of Torah-knowledge, he gained a large measure of piety. He himself subsequently became a shoemaker and was married through Reb Nissan's efforts coupled with the generous dowry Reb Tuvya bestowed on the bride. With his wife, Yisrael established a proud army of sons and sons-in-law who dedicated their lives to the study of Torah.

Old City veterans still remember Yisrael's shop in the Mydan *shuk*. They also recall how he would close his shop on Thursdays, take a large sack on his back and make the rounds to collect *challoth* and other Shabbath foods for the poorer families of the city.

This Yisrael was thus the end-product of the pure education of Reb Nissan the shoemaker, the vitality of Rav Shmuel Salant's holiness, and the vast wisdom of Rav Chayim Sonnenfeld — who later filled the post of Rav of Jerusalem.

And what became of the "deal" between Reb Tuvya and his Vilna benefactor, Reb Yona Tabak? That continued throughout their lifetime and was even perpetuated by their respective sons and grandsons for succeeding generations.

Even the Thinnest Thread

WHO WAS THIS Reb Nissan, the shoemaker who had the approval of all of Jerusalem's scholars, who had gained Rav Chayim's vote of confidence for his ability to educate, and to uproot the effects of Dr. Hertzberg's secularism?

Feiga, the bagel baker, a widow of several years, appeared one morning in the home of Rav Yehoshua Leib Diskin, the Brisker Rav. Her special plea was that he remember her only child, who had lain ill for several weeks, in his (holy) prayers. Rav Yehoshua Leib was distressed to hear of little Michel's illness. An unusually bright and endearing child, Michel had captivated many of Jerusalem's wise men who expected great things from this only son of the Brisker Rav's deceased star disciple. Rav Yehoshua Leib knew that the financial situation in the widow's house, difficult to begin with, must now be complicated by the boy's illness. He arose and paced the floor in his room, distraught, murmuring beseechingly half aloud, *"Ribono shel olam,* don't inflict both! Poverty and illness in one broken home is too much! *Ribono shel olam,* don't inflict both!"

Feiga's hold upon herself began to falter. Tears appeared in her eyes as she waited for the Rav's reply. After several minutes he turned to her saying, "Go and mention the boy to Reb Nissan the shoemaker."

Feiga's face wrinkled with worry, "Does the Rav really

think that my boy is so sick that Reb Nissan must pray for him?''

Reb Nissan was well-known in Jerusalem. His tiny shop, hidden in a dark alley and advertised by a hand-lettered sign that read, "Only Men's Shoes Fixed," had, despite its obscurity, become a well-known address. The Brisker Rav had seen to that.

Left with no choice, Feiga hurried to the alley where Reb Nissan's cubby-hole-within-a-cubby-hole shop was located, only to find it locked. When she asked the neighbors where he could possibly be, they shrugged their shoulders in reply and told her that the business had been closed all week long. This was nothing strange to Reb Nissan's usual customers, for he often locked up shop and disappeared from the public eye. Most of Reb Nissan's actions were, in fact, shrouded in mystery and secrecy. Nevertheless his absence this time seemed to be out of place in view of the unusual circumstances reigning in the city.

For it was not only Feiga who required Reb Nissan's unique services. The city of Jerusalem was suffering from a frightful typhoid epidemic at this time and the rabbinical courts had proclaimed a state of emergency which called for prayer and repentance. Now that the entire city needed Reb Nissan's valuable intercession he had seemingly vanished into the thin air.

Even his close friend and neighbor, Reb Shlomo Wexler, who studied with him in the Beith-El yeshiva for *mekubalim* began to worry. He sent his wife, Tzviya, to Reb Nissan's wife to find out where his friend could possibly be hiding, but Tzviya returned only with the information that Reb Nissan was out of town and would return within a few days.

"Out of town!? Outside of Jerusalem?" Reb Shlomo

gasped. "He has not stepped out of the city in all the years that he has lived here, ever since he immigrated here. Not even for an hour!"

"He most probably was sent by the Brisker Rav to fulfill some vital mission," Tzviya tried to calm her overwrought husband. "Aren't you the one who is always telling me that the Brisker Rav is the only man who appreciates Reb Nissan's full greatness and who utilizes it by assigning him all kinds of tasks involving the public welfare?"

Why, indeed, had Neb Nissan disappeared so mysteriously? And why had he violated his self-imposed confinement of forty years and left the holy city?

Reb Nisson's apartment flanked that of the pious and celebrated Reb Davidl Biderman.* The thin brick partition that separated the two flats somehow united the two great men who customarily spent their midnight-to-dawn hours in prayer and study respectively. On his side of the wall, Reb Nissan would recite a lengthy *tikkun chatzoth,* followed by an emotional recital of the entire Book of *Tehilim* and the *ma'amadoth* until the dawn signaled the hour for *vathikin* prayers. On the other side of the partition, Reb Davidl studied *Gemara* and *poskim* together with his friend Reb Manish Sheinberger.

In the quiet of the night Reb Davidl and Reb Manish could distinctly hear the plaintive voice of Reb Nissan mourning over the destruction and longing for the exiled Holy Presence. More than once their eyes had smarted and overflowed with hot tears in a sorrow shared by all Jews. As for Reb Nissan, how often had he clearly heard the discussions next door and taken a *gemara* in hand to follow

---

* Son of Rav El'azar Menachem Mendel and his successor as Rebbe of Lelov.

their dialectic. The wall-mates shared their nightly experiences but never acknowledged this fact to one another.

One night, while Reb Nissan was sitting on the hard ground, his head dusted with ashes, his lips declaiming the *tikkun chatzoth,* he overheard the lesson on the other side of his wall. The scholars were engaged in a discussion that involved the difficult section in *Gemara Beitza* concerning the prohibition of the *shaatnez* combination of linen and wool. The discussion seemed to him unusually loud and the words reached Reb Nissan distinctly and drew his interest. He took his small *gemara* and followed the conversation.

"Rabbi says in the name of the holy assembly of Jerusalem, 'It is prohibited to sleep on top of *kilayim* (*shaatnez*) even if ten mattresses are piled on top of the forbidden *shaatnez.'* "

Reb Nissan could hear Reb Davidl recite the Rambam's words of explanation: "The *kilayim* (*shaatnez*) prohibition has no minimum size or volume, even a single thread... He who sees *kilayim* as specified in the Torah (in a garment being worn) on his friend, even if the latter is walking in the marketplace, must pounce upon him and rip off the offending garment, even if that person be his own teacher..."

The night was a warm Tammuz one, of the kind that passes into early dawn before one realizes it. As dawn approached, Reb Davidl and Reb Manish left for the *mikveh* to purify themselves before their morning prayers in the *beith hamidrash* of the chassidim. Reb Nissan had preceeded them and was already leaving the *mikveh* to join his *vathikin minyan* at Yeshivath Beith-El. The neighbors met and exchanged a "Good morning." Then, suddenly and unaccountably, Reb Davidl stopped and began to review with Reb Nissan what he had learned that past

Rav Naftali Hertz Halevi, Rav of Jaffa

Reb Manish Sheinberger

night. He stated the *Gemara* in detail and expounded the Rambam on the *shaatnez* prohibition, that even if one saw his own teacher wearing *shaatnez* in the marketplace it was incumbent upon him to jump up and tear it off...

The neighbors then continued their separate ways, but Reb Yona Kornblit, the bathhouse attendant and a follower of Reb Davidl, could not help commenting upon his singular deviation from custom: this was the first time he had witnessed Reb Davidl speak before morning prayers!

Reb Nissan took his time with his davening. Shortly before noon he went to his little store to begin his work for the day. He made a quick survey of the shoes waiting to be repaired and a mental review of their owners. "It is only fitting for the honor of Torah that I mend the shoes of Torah scholars first," he decided and began to work upon the shoes of one of the Jerusalem *talmidey chachamim* with as much sacred dedication as he had devoted to reciting his prayers at night.

He was interrupted in the midst of his labor by an Arab peddler who was offering to sell fifteen pairs of wool-lined boots from Damascus for an unheard-of bargain price. Reb Nissan pounced happily upon this opportunity and speedily completed the transaction. *Fifteen pairs of Jerusalem feet will not suffer this coming winter, thanks to this timely purchase,* he reflected joyfully.

After another half-hour Reb Nissan was interrupted again, this time by a customer. A long-bearded, distinguished-looking Jew passing by had noticed the boots standing in the entrance of the shop, and was interested in buying himself a pair. After a brief exchange, the Jew was provided with a pair of boots his size, wrapped up and now all his. Reb Nissan took stock of the profit he had earned within such a short time and decided that the sum was equal to a whole day's labor. He thanked his customer for the business and then asked as an afterthought.

"Where do you come from?"

"I am from Jaffa," the stranger replied, and left the shop.

Having earned enough for one day's living expenses, Reb Nissan arose and, closing his store, headed for the *beith ha-midrash*. He sat down and began to study but found to his dismay that he could not concentrate upon the words of his *seifer*. Instead, Reb Davidl's words kept coming back to him. Not only the words, but Reb Davidl's very voice and Reb Manish's answering voice kept ringing in his ears. "Even ten mattresses piled one above the other, under which *kilayim* is present, is prohibited ... *Kilayim* has no minimum measurement, even one single thread. . ."

"What has happened to me?" Reb Nisson wondered. "I have been overhearing Reb Davidl's midnight lessons for years now and they have never haunted me thus in the daytime!" Reb Nissan gathered his thoughts together and tried attacking his *seifer* once more but again found his mind wandering from the page. Now he saw before him Reb Davidl entering the *mikveh* courtyard and stopping to review with him what he had learned the night before. The two had long been neighbors, yet never before had Reb Davidl stopped him in the morning to discuss what he had studied the previous night!

Suddenly something dawned upon Reb Nissan. As if struck by a thunderbolt, he recalled the wool-lined boots he had purchased that morning. They must have been sewn with a linen thread, he deduced, which was why Reb Davidl had so explicitly expounded the laws of *shaatnez*. Reb Davidl had surely foreseen this in his holy vision.

Reb Nissan closed his *seifer* and davened *mincha* quickly

with one of the *minyanim* in the Churva. Then he hurried
to his store, loaded the sack of boots on his shoulder and
ran to Reb Chayim Singer, the *shaatnez* expert who lived
in the courtyard adjoining the Torath Chayim yeshiva
near the Damascus Gate. Knowing the importance of his
visitor, Reb Chayim wished to give him a speedy reply
and so he quickly took out the tools of his trade, his
needles and his magnifying glass, and set to work. After
a thorough, expert examination, Reb Chayim announced,
"*Shaatnez.* Completely *shaatnez.*"

Reb Nissan was thoroughly agitated. Grabbing the culprit sack he left the room without a parting word, and ran
as quickly as his shaking legs could carry him to the
Brisker Rav.

Looking like a peddler with his sack on his shoulder,
Reb Nissan entered Rav Yehoshua Leib's house. Dejectedly, he explained how he had sold a pair of *shaatnez*
boots to a stranger from Jaffa, thereby transgressing the
Torah prohibition stating, "Do not place a stumbling
block before the blind." He then informed the Brisker
Rav of his intention to set out for Jaffa on the morrow
to seek the stranger who had bought his boots.

Rav Yehoshua Leib did not give the decision halachic
sanction but he blessed the shoemaker with a curt, "May
God help you."

When the next day dawned it found Reb Nissan on an
express wagon headed for Jaffa. Throughout the journey
he kept urging the driver to make all possible haste. They
finally reached their destination toward evening. Reb
Nissan alighted and stretched his aching legs on the burning sands of Jaffa, a city that was completely strange
to him. He was looking for someone who could give him
a slight clue, an inkling of where to find the Jew who had
purchased the *shaatnez* boots. After a short walk he met

someone whom he asked for the location of a *shul,* upon which the local resident returned his greeting and took him to a parallel street where stood the main synagogue of the city. Reb Nissan caught a *minyan* in the courtyard outside and a between-*mincha*-and-*maariv shi'ur* inside in *Mishnayoth* for the seventy-odd tradesmen and merchants, delivered by the Rav of the city, Rav Naftali Hertz Halevi.

Rav Naftali, who was an avid admirer and devoted disciple of the Brisker Rav, recognized Reb Nissan as soon as he entered, and rose to his full height. Who sees his own Rav standing up for someone without standing up in turn? And so the whole congregation paid its respects to the poor cobbler who seemed just that and no more. Reb Nissan hurried to hide behind the stove as if the Rav had made some embarrassing mistake but after *maariv* Rav Naftali went over to the humble guest, shook his hand and embraced him warmly.

The *gabbai* of the synagogue, Reb Ezra Saperstein, could barely contain his impatience. He had learned meanwhile that the respected visitor was, in fact, no more than a poor Jerusalem cobbler. Why did he merit such a show of feeling from the Rav? He approached Rav Naftali and asked him point blank.

"I really cannot tell you much about the man," the Rav confessed, "but I can attest that Rav Yehoshua Leib, my teacher and mentor, averred that this Reb Nissan is a true *tzaddik nistar,* an unrevealed *tzaddik* of our generation."

Reb Naftali went over to Reb Nissan again, and this time invited him to dine in his home and explain what brought him to Jaffa. Not wishing to refuse, Reb Nissan accompanied the Rav home, where a festive table was laid out in honor of the important guest. As soon as he saw the array. Reb Nissan burst into tears. He launched into the story that had brought him to Jaffa, explaining how he had been the stumbling-block for a Jaffa Jew.

"Please help me locate this man so that I may save him from a terrible sin," he begged his host urgently.

"Did you tell this story to our *rebbi*, the Brisker Rav?" Rav Naftoli inquired.

"Surely. He even blessed my mission."

"Well, then," the Rav calmed the upset man, "you have nothing to worry about. I am certain that God will bless your mission with success."

Rav Naftali's son-in-law, Rav Yosef Tzvi Halevi, who filled his father-in-law's post in later years, was a witness to this scene. He could not contain his wonder. "What fantastic piety! What astounding fear of God! How does one attain such a degree of perfection?" he whispered all agog.

Reb Nissan had arrived in Jaffa on a Monday. Three days passed and still no sign of his unfortunate customer. Reb Nissan's agitation, which grew from day to day, was barely allayed by Rav Naftali's repeated assurances that their *rebbi's* blessing would be fulfilled.

On Thursday, after *shacharith*, the *shamash* of the *shul* came to the Rav with a request. That day had been set for a *chalitza* ceremony for a Jew who had come from abroad. Since the *beith din* courtroom was presently undergoing repairs, the *shamash* asked the Rav to be so obliging as to have the ceremony in his home, to which the Rav readily agreed.

The *chalitza* took place some two hours later and Reb Nissan was witness to it too. When it was all over and the crowd had begun to disperse, the visitor from Jerusalem suddenly spied a familiar face. As quick as a wink he was by the man's side.

Rav Yosef Tzvi Halevi

*Part of a letter from Rav Naftali Hertz to Rav Naftali Tzvi
Berlin of Volozhin*

"Weren't you in Jerusalem this week?" he asked, his heart pounding.

"Yes," the man verified, adding as an afterthought, "and aren't you the cobbler from the Old City?"

Reb Nissan burst into tears once again, but these were tears of joy and relief.

Rav Naftali, witnessing this brief scene, also burst into tears for his *rebbi's* blessing had been completely realized.

Reb Nissan returned on the following day, boots in hand, to his native city, to resume his daily routine of study, toil, and prayer.

Truly then, it was no arbitrary choice of the Jerusalem *rabbanim* to entrust the education of a precious Jewish soul that had been snatched away from spiritual perdition — the soul of this boy Yisraelka — to the hands of this simple, yet not so simple, cobbler.

BOOK
2

ירושלים של מעלה

Inside
the Daily Lives
of Jerusalem Jewry

Prayer at the Kothel

WHEN TROUBLES BEFALL the community, people's personal problems seem to vanish.

The months of Cheshvan and Kislev had passed. It was Teveth and rain had still not fallen in Jerusalem. The ground was dry, parched, and cracked. The sun blazed Tammuz-like and all living things, man and animal, cried out for water. The city was plagued with epidemics of all kinds, including typhoid, which took a heavy toll of lives.

Water could be gotten, but for a price. The Arabs transported water in leather gourds strapped to their donkeys' backs from the wells near the site of the *Mikdash* and they charged exorbitantly for every precious drop of it. Each morning the Jerusalem women stood on line to buy a canful of water each, waiting their turns in the blazing sun. The suffering was great; it was tragic.

The Rav, Rav Shmuel Salant, summoned the pious and learned members of the rabbinical courts and other wise men of the city to his home to discuss what measures they should take to nullify the harsh Heavenly decree.

The great men decided to proclaim the coming *erev* Rosh Chodesh Shvat as a day of fasting, prayer, and repentance climaxed by a *mincha* service at the Kothel haMaaravi. This *mincha* was to be attended by all the *cheider*-children of the city who would keynote the event with their pure prayers requesting the much-needed rain.

A proclamation, signed by all the rabbis who had attended the meeting, went out to the entire city. On the evening preceding the fast, the *shamash* of the *beith din* went forth to proclaim, in his thundering voice, that the morrow would be a day of fasting and prayer.

On the following day the *shuls* of the Chassidim, Perushim, Sefaradim, and Ashkenazim were all brimful with worshipers reciting *Tehilim* and *selichoth* without pause. Later that afternoon the *shuls* and the houses emptied simultaneously, and the streets filled with people streaming in one direction, to the Kothel haMaaravi. Thousands filled the square in front of the Kothel and all roads, alleys, and passageways leading up to it were black with heads upon which the sun beat relentlessly. A veritable sea of faces was uplifted to heaven.

The thousands of *cheider*-boys streaming toward the Kothel added a poignant, even frightening tone to the already stirring spectacle. Group by group, they proceeded, each boy with a *Tehilim* under his arm, each group led by its *melamed*, the groups piloted by Rav Shmuel Salant's *shamash* proclaiming in his resounding voice that the streets be cleared for the *'tinokoth shel beith raban.'*

The little figures neared the Kothel and the packed area directly in front of it was willingly cleared for them.

Rav Nota Weiss, the *maggid*, engulfed in his *tallith*, stepped forward. Beside him stood the Rav of Brisk's famous *shofar* blowers, each with his *shofar* ready in hand. Rav Nota began by leading the crowd in reciting *Tehilim*, verse by verse. After each chapter he said a special *Yehi Ratzon* prayer followed by recital of the Thirteen Attributes of Divine Mercy and the awesome blasts of the Ashkenazic and Sefaradic *shofars.* When they had completed the *Tehilim,* Rav Nota began to recite *E-l na refa na tachalu'ay geffen poriya* in a tear-choked voice, and thousands of supplicating voices reverberated in response.

*A group praying beside the Western Wall on the eve of
Rosh Chodesh*

Jews of Jerusalem on their way to the Western Wall

The *selichoth* completed, Rav Nota climbed up on a high stool and began to address the crowd with moving words, asking each person, in the name of all the great rabbis of the Holy City, to examine his own soul to see if anything was wanting and to repent fully then and there.

His words evoked tears, moans, and cries. But all of a sudden the tightly packed crowd seethed with a different sound. Cries of "Make way!" became audible from the far edges of the assemblage.

Rav Shneyer Zalman of Lublin — the eminent author of *Torath Chessed,* who had immigrated to Eretz Yisrael in his later years — was approaching. An awesome, great revered figure, the Rav of Lublin spent his days secluded at home, immersed in prayer and study. To the great surprise of his household, he had announced his intention of attending the *mincha* services at the Kothel despite his weakness due to the fast and his advanced age. That surprise was tempered by concern. But the next surprise was total, and left them open-mouthed. The Rav of Lublin left his home wearing his heavy fur winter hat.

The awesome figure trudged slowly toward the Kothel in the suffocating heat. As he passed through the Arab marketplace, between the rows of Arabs smoking their drug-filled pipes and reclining in a semi-trance on the ground, a strange thing happened. The languid Arabs arose to full stature and bowed as he passed between them. "That's the Jewish Chacham," they whispered reverently to one another. "He will bring the rains."

From his vantage point on the stool, Rav Nota caught sight of the *gaon* approaching and he grew flustered with awe of the Torah-master. He quickly finished his message, dropped off his improvised podium, and motioned to the *chazan* to proceed with *mincha.*

It was an emotion-packed *mincha*, mingled with plentiful

tears. When the *chazan* reached *Boreich oleinu,* he was interrupted by hundreds of youthful voices chanting the verse *"Vethein tal umatar."* These were the children of the Sefaradi schools who said the verse over and over again. They were joined by the childish trebles of the Ashkenazi boys who cried out the verse in a rising crescendo of emotion that went on and on. The young congregation must have said the verse thirty times — the children imploring, the adults weeping — before their teachers succeeded in stilling their insistent voices in order to let the *chazan* continue to the end of the *bracha.* The resounding "Amein" that greeted the *bracha* must surely have sent it thundering straight into heaven.

Mincha was followed by *maariv,* after which the throngs slowly dispersed to return home. The Rav of Lublin began his homeward trek with slow steps, followed by a huge crowd of people who walked after him, step by step. They were part way up the hill to Batey Machseh when the skies grew overcast and then quickly darkened with thick black clouds. A fierce thunderbolt rattled the air, and within seconds a gushing rain fell heavily earthward. The heavenly floodgates had been unlocked.

"A guten chodesh," the crowd yelled happily as, drenched to the bone, they reached the home of the Rav of Lublin, "A good month, *rebbe."* Overcome by joy. they pressed his hand and kissed it reverently as they parted and ran to find shelter from the pouring rain that lashed at their faces and penetrated the cracked earth. The wells and cisterns that had stood empty for so many months now filled quickly with life-giving liquid and the Jews of Jerusalem sang praises to the Holy One, blessed is He.

The Child's Prayer

No ONE HAD NOTICED the absence of Reb Velvel Chevroner
— the well-known man of good deeds — at the mass
Kothel haMaaravi prayer gathering. Reb Velvel was a man
who never removed himself from matters of public concern, so his absence should have aroused some questions.
But then, who could determine who had been present at
the Kothel and who not? Thousands of Jews had participated in that memorable gathering but many Yerushalmim
had gone to prostrate themselves upon the grave of the
saintly Or HaChayim on the Mount of Olives instead,
and could not, therefore, have been present at the Kothel
prayers.

The one person who did feel Reb Velvel's absence was
Reb Muttel Trup, who lived on Jews' Street in the Old
City. Reb Muttel Trup was a simple, everyday Jew. Born
in a secluded village in the Carpathian Mountains, Reb
Muttel was orphaned of his peasant father at the tender
age of four. His mother supported the two of them with
difficulty but squeezed from her meager income enough to
pay for a *melamed* to teach her son the rudiments of
Chumash. The *melamed* soon found himself a more lucra-
tive position, and moved away from that secluded village
and from the unfortunate orphan. As a result, the boy's
knowledge never went beyond *Ein Yaakov* and *Sheivet
Mussar* with Yiddish translation, but his piety by far
surpassed his knowledge.

When he grew to young adulthood, Muttel immigrated to Eretz Yisrael with his old mother, settling in Jaffa. There he married and became a monument engraver at the Jaffa cemetery. Reb Muttel plied his trade honestly; he kept his hands busy and his mouth free from evil gossip or idle talk. He served God to the best of his humble knowledge, believing in Him with a naive, trustful, serene love. He lived thus until one incident, which remained a personal secret throughout Muttel's lifetime, caused him to change his entire lifestyle.

It happened that a freethinking and totally irreligious Jew passed away. The deceased's family came to Reb Muttel to order a monument for his grave, specifying a whole wreathful of glorious titles and epithets of honor. The honest Reb Muttel refused to execute such a tombstone, and his honesty cost him his job. The city council relieved him of his post and Reb Muttel was forced to relocate in Jerusalem.

Reb Muttel was blessed with one son, Feitel, who learned in the Etz Chayim *cheider*. The boy's teachers predicted a bright future for Feitel when he was only five years old. Like many of his *cheider*-mates, *Feitel* contracted typhoid during the difficult days of the drought. When the proclaimed fast day arrived, his father, Reb Muttel, was among the thousands of worshippers at the Kothel, for he wished to add a personal prayer for his son's speedy recovery. Reb Muttel's pious wife also wished to pour out her prayers at the holy site but dared not leave her sick son alone. Her one recourse was to beg her good neighbor, the man who never refused anyone a favor, to watch the boy for a short while until she returned. Reb Velvel Chevroner, indeed, did not refuse, and, accompanied by his *Tehilim*, sat by the bedside of the ailing Feitel. Once there, he began a non-stop flow of

Tehilim and prayers for the boy, for the rains, and for the living and growing things.

What happened next was a story that Reb Velvel Chevroner would repeat many, many times. As he sat praying by the boy's bedside, Feitel suddenly awoke from his semi-delirium, and with his emaciated hand held to his head so that his *yarmulka* would not slip off, he gathered all his strength into a simple prayer of his own.

"*Ribono shel olam*," he breathed, "give us some rain already. Give us rain. Our cistern is empty. My mother cries; I also cry. Why do we have so little water to wash our hands for *netilath yadayim*? Please, please send us rain so that I will be able to wash my hands with lots of water..."

A dream-prayer of a five-year-old boy, but it, too, surely rose heavenward to join the prayers of the Jerusalem community.

And when Reb Velvel Chevroner later repeated the boy's prayer to the saintly Rav Meshel Gelbstein, the latter reacted by pronouncing, "The boy's words were not a product of the delirium of typhoid fever, they were the outcome of a fever of piety inculcated in him by his God-fearing mother and father from the time of his birth!"

The boy was five years old in all and yet he knew the fine points of the halachic observance in washing his hands as well as an adult. This was not surprising, actually, since his father had washed Feitel's hands every single morning of the boy's life from the eighth day on!

And indeed, Feitel matured to become a young Torah scholar renowned for his piety and knowledge. So celebrated was he that the Rebbe of Lelov, Rav El'azar Mendel of Jerusalem — acclaimed by all as a *tzaddik* whose every action embodied holiness and upon whom God's

Holy Spirit rested — one day stood up to pay this young scholar homage.

Rav El'azar Mendel, it is also said, once expressed his esteem in a succinct phrase, "This young man has pure eyes." A short phrase, it said a lot.

The Rav of Piotrkov Visits Jerusalem

"ALL THE DAYS of the poor man are bad," said the sage ben-Sira. This pithy saying held steadfastly true for Reb Feitel, son of Reb Muttel Trup, who lived on the slope of Chabad Street in a small apartment, or what passed for an apartment, with his wife and six children.

During the summer, when the sun beat down, it was unbearably hot in the house. The kitchen — a shed covered by a tin roof — heated up like an oven and the apartment itself grew so infernal that anyone not accustomed to such heat could not suffer it for a moment. And in winter, when Jerusalem was blessed with rain, the house was again unlivable. As if it were a special target for the rains, the apartment would flood with water which seeped in under the threshold. Wetness was absorbed by the walls and would leak out onto the floor. Poor Breindel, Feitel's good wife, would have to bail out pailful after pailful of water into the nearby cistern to prevent it from seeping back into the house through the soaked ground.

The Jews of Jerusalem, especially Reb Feitel's fellow-scholars, were not surprised that their friend never complained about his lot. To a man who knew by heart the chapter entitled "The Gate of Confidence in God" from the *Chovoth haLevavoth*, what could material comfort signify? Were his living quarters not, after all, temporary ones compared to the eternal home one had waiting for him in the world of eternal good?

Nothing surprising in that at all. What was surprising was that his wife, Breindel, also felt that way. She, too, never complained about her lot, never demanded that he improve their apartment or exchange it for a better, more spacious one. Whenever her neighbors brought up the subject, or advised her to insist that her husband provide better living conditions, she would answer complacently, "Compared with my father's home, may he rest in peace, this is a veritable palace." And she would seize the opportunity to tell them about her saintly father, grandson of Rav Yeshaya Haleivi Horowitz, Rav of Frankfurt and Prague, known as the "Shaloh haKadosh."* He had lived in cramped quarters indeed, but then he had had no need for more than four square cubits. His house never boasted four matching chairs.

"Who am I and what is my life to compare with my father, that I should require more?" Breindel would say. And then she would add, "As long as my husband can continue his Torah study without interruption, I ask for nothing more." Thus would she end the conversation.

Sometimes, when her neighbors persisted, she would answer them with a story. The story centered around a *talmid chacham* in the city of Suvalk, Breindel's birthplace. His wife persistently pestered her husband to find them better living quarters. When he could stand her constant nagging no longer, he contracted a loan to finance a move to a more spacious apartment. As a result, he became heavily indebted and was forced to quit his studies, after which he was never able to resume them fully again.

---

* *Shaloh* is an acronym formed from the initial letters of his classic work, *Shenay Luchoth Habrith.*

He subsequently forgot most of what he had learned and agonized over his loss to the end of his days.

No one really knew on what Reb Feitel and his family lived. He never took the monthly stipend offered by the yeshiva and yet he was a full-time yeshiva scholar all his days and throughout every day. Mornings he would be seen studying *Shulchan Aruch* with Rav Hirsh Michel Shapiro. Afternoons he would spend an intensive study period with the famous Rav Zevulun Charlap of the *beith din,* and evenings he would study with his children and review what they had learned. Early every morning he would be in the Or haChayim's synagogue with the scholarly Rav Yaakov Orenstein, engrossed in the laws pertaining to the Holy Land.

When and how did he manage to earn a livelihood?

Feitel's wife, Breindel, was related to the Rav of Piotrkov and later of Kalish in Poland, Rav Chayim El'azar Wax. The latter was well aware that his relative in Jerusalem was a Torah-giant and an extremely modest young man; the charity representatives of the various institutions in the Holy City would rave about Reb Feitel's character and greatness whenever they visited Piotrkov. Consequently, Rav Chayim El'azar undertook to support the young man in such manner as to enable him to live comfortably. The Rav of Piotrkov reason thus: The Etz Chayim yeshiva certainly gave Reb Feitel a monthly stipend. Since this stipend is most probably not enough to make ends meet, he would supplement it with an additional monthly sum which would enable him to study Torah without financial worries. True to his decision, Rav Chayim El'azar regularly sent Reb Feitel a monthly check which amounted to approximately half the sum allocated to yeshiva scholars by the Etz Chayim yeshiva. Each month Reb Feitel would send a lengthy letter of acknowledgement to his benefactor, replete with his Torah-*chidushim*. The Rav of Piotrkov would read these letters with a satisfying feeling that his money was helping support a true Torah scholar. So this arrangement was continued for seven years, until the Rav of Piotrkov came to Jerusalem and stopped the stipend.

At the end of seven years the Rav of Piotrkov visited the Holy City and stopped in to pay his respects at the home of Rav Shmuel Salant. Their conversation turned to Reb Feitel Trup, and Rav Chayim El'azar boasted about his young relative's Torah scholarship, the comprehensiveness and astuteness that he enjoyed so much in the monthly letters he received. To prove his point, he pulled some recent letters out of his pocket and showed them to Rav Shmuel, who pored over them for a quarter of an hour, ohing and ahing over their contents, muttering to himself in sheer surprise. "Wonderful! Marvelous! I never dreamed that Reb Feitel's knowledge was so extensive! I knew him for the *tzaddik* he is, for his humility, but that he incorporates and hides such Torah greatness too!"

"Why do you call him such an outstanding *tzaddik*?" the European *Rav* asked curiously. "I know him to be an outstanding scholar, but now you tell me he is outstanding in his piety as well. How is it that you never realized all all these years how great his Torah wisdom was?"

"Simple," his host answered. "To me he doesn't send his Torah thoughts and I never engage him in scholarly discussions. How then should I know the treasures he hides? As for his being a *tzaddik* — that speaks for itself in his ability to hide the extent of his Torah-knowledge!"

"If this is true," Rav Chayim El'azar ventured, addressing Rav Shmuel respectfully in the third person, "then might I be so bold as to suggest to the Rav of Jerusalem, who is simultaneously the Dean of the Etz Chayim yeshiva, that Reb Feitel receive a raise in view of his six children and that house he lives in. . ."

"A raise?" Rav Shmuel wondered. "Based on what?"

"On the money that the yeshiva pays him."

"What money?"

"The money he gets from Etz Chayim!"

"But he never gets any."

"What!" Rav Chayim El'azar exclaimed in disbelief, "Reb Feitel doesn't receive money from the yeshiva?"

"No, and he never did. I, myself, spoke to him about it a short while ago, but he continued to refuse to take any."

"I have no idea what the matter is with my Reb Feitel," the Polish rabbi exclaimed in exasperated puzzlement as he rose and ended the visit.

When Reb Feitel and his family went to visit their uncle on the following day, Rav Chayim El'azar accosted the young man directly, "Tell me, Reb Feitel, tell me, what do you live on?"

"Ahem," Reb Feitel hesitated, wringing his thin hands nervously. "The gracious Rav of Piotrkov sends us money every month. . ."

"And besides that?" the older man asked with a show of severity.

"Besides that? That is enough." Reb Feitel breathed confusedly.

"And what about the yeshiva allotment?"

Reb Feitel twisted uncomfortably, lowering his eyes in shame as if he had been caught in a crime. He did not have the courage to answer his uncle and enter into an argument with him.

Seeing his plight, Breindel took his part and begged her uncle to let her speak for them both. He did.

"My husband refuses to take yeshiva money," she explained. "He fears that by taking from the yeshiva he reduces the amount the other poor scholars have to divide, and they don't have uncles abroad who send them money each month as you do."

"And thank God for that," she continued gratefully. "We have enough to eat and drink, and there is no cause to pity us. But may I beg you now to bless our children that we might see *nachas* from them," she requested, motioning to the children who stood off to the side. "Bless them that they should follow in their father's footsteps. Moshe Hillel, Hershel, David Nachman, Shmulik," she summoned them. "Come here and let the Rav give you a *bracha*."

The boys approached their great-uncle who laid his hands upon their small heads and blessed them one by one, tears of emotion welling in his eyes. Then he turned to Reb Feitel, "I always thought that I was doing you a favor with the money I sent you. I thought that the seven years during which you received my monthly allotment were seven years of plenty. Now I learn that they were seven years of hunger. With this knowledge, I find it superfluous, even detrimental, to continue sending the money directly to you and have you starve. Instead I will send it straight to the yeshiva and you will draw a monthly stipend together with the other yeshiva scholars. That way you will be getting twice what you were getting all along, and will at least be on the same footing as other yeshiva families."

"God forbid," Reb Feitel answered in an injured tone, at the same time springing up to defend himself. "You did me a favor all these past years and you did a favor to the yeshiva as well, a real favor. . ."

When the Rav of Piotrkov returned home he related

this story to his friends. "Let it be known that we don't have even the slightest conception of what Jerusalem has hidden away. I myself did not know of its treasures until I saw with my own eyes."

When these words got back to Rav Shmuel Salant, he commented in passing, "So the Rav of Piotrkov thinks he has already seen everything Jerusalem has?"

Luxury in Jerusalem of Yesteryear

AND INDEED, the Rav of Piotrkov could not possibly have seen all there was to see in the Holy City. During his stay he did manage to meet many of the city's favored sons and he viewed throngs of precious Jews passing through Jerusalem's streets and side streets, but it is doubtful if he was able to see through to their inner souls, to their previous essence. He could clearly see that Jerusalem harbored personalities that burned with fiery zeal. Yet there were other Jews who were not the scholars and wise men the city was famous for, but common folk whose inner souls were difficult to penetrate. The giants of the spirit belonged in a class by themselves. Surely God had specifically planted them in the Holy City to shield and protect the entire generation. But Jerusalem's "simple" folk — the tailors, cobblers, jokesters, and "idlers" — they concealed virtues that one got only rare glimpses of.

One important Yerushalmi celebrated his son's wedding and honored the Rav of Piotrkov with conducting the *kiddushin* ceremony. That was how he came to attend the wedding dinner that took place later in the home of the *chathan*'s father in Batey Machseh.

The two Jerusalem *badchanim*, Reb Dan Pleitzes and Reb Koppel Dropkin, stood for four hours on end on a table in the center of the room, their drums tied around their necks and dangling upon their chests. They sang; they danced; they beat their drums; they joked and entertained the *chathan* and *kalla* with their amusing antics until past midnight.

What impression could these pranksters possibly leave on the celebrated guests other than that of clowns or buffoons?

It didn't occur to any of the wedding participants to explain to the Rav of Piotrkov that these *badchanim* actually were replete with Torah, mitzvos, charitable deeds, and piety. It didn't strike anyone to whisper to the visitor that if he went to the Rabbi Yochanan ben Zakkai *shul* after midnight he would find these very "clowns" sitting and studying together until dawn. Even after four strenuous hours of entertaining others!

When their talents were not required, the two men would study together after *ma'ariv* until midnight. But when there was a wedding in town, especially a wedding of poor people, they would go to amuse the *chathan* and *kalla* until midnight, and postpone their daily study period until after midnight, studying until daylight. Whenever morning worshippers would meet Reb Dan and Reb Koppel at the *vathikin davvening*, they could deduce that a wedding had been celebrated the night before.

A heavy snow once fell in Jerusalem. It covered the face of the city and for a whole week people did not dare venture outside. Only these two trudged from house to house giving out bread and doling out warm milk to young children.

When the *gaon* Rav Akiva Yosef Schlesinger spied them from his window carrying heavy sacks of food on their backs, he called out to them, "I am certain that you are genuine *olam-haba* people."

Did it occur to the Rav of Piotrkov that the young, thin milkman whose hair fell into his eyes and whose

*A group of badchanim who entertained at Jerusalem
weddings of those days*

The synagogue of Rabbi Yochanan Ben Zakkai

clothes were held together by patched patches — the one who delivered fresh goats' milk each morning — was another of Jerusalem's supersouls? A man who knew all the tractates of *Kodashim* by heart, the milkman was a scholar who regularly studied the tractate *Zevachim* with the eminent old sage, Rav Avraham Shag of Kaubersdorf. Actually this young scholar was not a milkman at all. He was only substituting for the regular milkman who had contracted pneumonia and could not support his family. And this young scholar-milkman worked as a replacement throughout the man's illness without accepting any fee whatever!

No, the Rav of Piotrkov did not know half these things.

One day the visiting scholar was walking down a Jerusalem street. Spying a young boy running past, a *gemara Bava Metzia* under one arm and a paper bag under the other, he stopped him with a gentle pat on the cheek and asked the child,

"What are you carrying in your bag?"

"Lunch for the *cheider*," was the succinct reply.

The Rav was in a good mood and his curiosity led him to ask permission to examine the contents of that paper bag. The boy recognized the stranger from a visit he had paid the *cheider* and agreed. The Rav peeked inside and found two pieces of black bread stuck together with some oil and a slice of herring. Roused to pity by such frugal fare, he led the boy to the nearest store where he bought some tomatoes and threw them into the bag. The boy then continued running to *cheider*.

Did the Rav ever find out that the boy never ate the tomatoes, but instead gave them to the poor Persian beggar who sat by the *cheider* entrance? The boy's father had repeatedly explained that luxuries are forbidden and, since the child understood that his meal could be eaten without tomatoes, that vegetable constituted a luxury!

While in Jerusalem, Rav Chayim El'azar discussed a business deal. He planned the printing of his work *Nefesh Chaya* with one Reb Zimmel, a printer. Little did the visitor suspect that his printer, a plain looking man who for some reason or other covered his head with a tarbush winter and summer, could have been a wealthy man with a prosperous business had he accepted the business that Nissim Bachar had offered him. Bachar, the principal of a secular school affiliated with the *Alliance Israélite Universelle* movement, tempted Reb Zimmel with handsome fees and a promise of business to print his educational material. Reb Zimmel dutifully asked the Jerusalem *rabbanim* before accepting and, when they forbade the printing of such freethinking literature, withstood the temptation, choosing instead to live a life of semi-starvation rather than disobey his rabbis. And who was this man after all? Just another of Jerusalem's simple folk, a mere tradesman!

No wonder then that Nissim Bachar wrote to his sponsors abroad a letter of exasperation and defeat. "They are stronger than we are. We will never overcome them."

A Single Tear

"...TAKE IT EASY, Friend Bachar. Take your time with the Jerusalem Jews. They are adamant; they are granite. They adhere to their tradition; they cling to their rabbis, especially to Rabbi Diskin of Brisk whose figure commands the awe of the entire Old Yishuv settlement. Be advised that we will not free the education in the Old City from the power of these rabbis in one day. Continue to proceed slowly, with restraint. With this in mind you must continue to educate the students in the Lemel school under your supervision with some practical religious commandments that you may deceive the public. Hand in hand with these religious practices you can teach them secular sciences, languages, nationalism, pioneer spirit, love of the land, and thus, bit by bit, you will attract new students, one boy after another, one girl after another. Via this gradual process we will in the end achieve our aims of dominating the field of education in Jerusalem, and if we have that in our hands then we have the entire settlement under our control. The main thing is not to lose hope; the funds are at your disposal and our good friend Mr. Pines is at your right hand to promote the success of your undertaking with his prolific abilities. Do not lend an ear to the shofar blasts emanating from the courtrooms of the Rabbi of Brisk and his disciples. Forget his condemnations. Do not react to his declaration of war against you, for that will only strengthen them."

120

This could have been a letter written by the directors of the *Alliance Israélite Universelle* in Paris to their representative in Eretz Yisrael, Nissim Bachar, in reply to a letter of despair in which he expressed his weariness over the impossible task entrusted to him of introducing modern education into the holy city.

Bachar took the advice and rallied again to his mission, beginning modestly with a handful of children, most of them orphans or children from impoverished Sefaradi homes. In the framework of the Lemel school these children were educated in selected practical religious commandments. They all wore *tzitzith* on their clothing, skullcaps on their heads. They were often seen in the course of the year, going out at night together with their instructors to bless the new moon. And these various camouflages succeeded to a large degree.

The Godfearing Yerushalmim, however, were not taken in. They ingested the stringent rabbinical ban on all the secular schools into their blood. The faithful Jews kept their distance from the school, from fear of being poisoned by it.

Among these was Reb Yoel Ehrentreu who immigrated to Eretz Yisrael in his youth from his native Serdahely, Hungary, where he had studied under the great *gaon* Rav Yehuda Assad. His home was just a short distance from the Lemel school.

Reb Yoel had three daughters, all married to Yerushalmi Torah scholars of repute. Whenever his daughters visited him, the elderly Reb Yoel would sit them down at the table and review with them the letter of the ban on the secular schools, translating it word for word into popular Yiddish. The fervor and intensity he applied to this lecture soon caused his daughters to know it by heart.

Reb Yoel continued this practice until his death shortly

after World War One in 5678 (1918). He left a brief will to his grandchildren, begging them to inscribe upon his tombstone the following words: "He opposed Zionism with all his might throughout his life."

Very few of Reb Yoel's acquaintances knew the secret behind this violent opposition. Here and there someone from among the inner circle of frequent visitors who came to listen to his tales about the famous rabbis and teachers that had influenced him in Europe, knew the truth. Reb Yoel's fanatic zeal was the product of one tear, one pure soul-drop that fell from the Rav of Brisk's saintly eye.

Rav Yehoshua Leib Diskin once gathered together the communal leaders of Jerusalem. He expounded on the severity of the ban on entering the hall which Michel Pines erected in the Evven Yisrael section to tempt Jewish souls into exchanging their traditions for progressiveness. When Rav Yehoshua Leib described the pain that the Divine Presence felt, as it were, and when he elaborated on the great danger that imperiled Jerusalem education, a single blood-tear fell and seared deeply into Reb Yoel's soul and into the souls of all those present. That hot tear still stung and boiled in loyal Jewish hearts even many years later.

It is no small wonder then that Reb Yoel, who was among the select assembly on that memorable occasion, was deeply affected by that seething drop until the end of his days. He kept the sacredness of the ban; he studied its words repeatedly with his daughters and grandchildren so that its impact would not lessen with the coming generations but would be freshly preserved and potent until the coming of Mashiach. During the course of the year, Reb Yoel and his family had no contact with their neighbors, the school and its instructors. Whenever Reb Yoel left or entered his home he would skirt that establishment, giving it a wide berth to fulfill the Torah's commandment, "And you shall not venture near her doorway." He interpreted "her" as heresy, and what could be more heretical than subverting the minds of Jewish children with atheism and apostasy?

And so Reb Yoel managed to avoid any clashes, until a time when circumstances made a clash inevitable. Though Reb Yoel was fully prepared to sacrifice his life for his principles, the clash, fortunately, did not cost any lives.

True to the *Alliance* principle of maintaining outward appearances, the school celebrated Sukkoth with a *sukka*, much as they celebrated Chanuka with latkes, Passover with *kneidlach,* Purim with masquerade and feasting, and Shavuoth with greens. One year they decided to expand their usual *sukka* threefold in order to accommodate some guests from abroad whom they wished to fete during the holiday. They extended their *sukka* until it actually reached Reb Yoel's and utilized one of his walls, which they intended to call their own on its other side.

As is the custom of good Jews, Reb Yoel had begun his *sukka* right after Yom Kippur, and he completed its construction on the morrow. The school began theirs on the very day of *erev* Sukkoth, with all of the students participating. Reb Yoel became aware of the defilement of his *sukka* shortly before the holiday actually set in, just as he was leaving his home for the *mikveh.* He saw that the students had relied upon his *sukka* wall to form one of their walls and feared that he might be violating the rabbinical ban against having any form of contact with the secular institution. This was contact in the flesh!

Reb Yoel's distress was indescribable, but the lateness of the hour forced him to continue on to the *mikveh.* Halfway there he met Rav Zorach Braverman to whom he poured out his tale of woe, explaining how he would be forced to celebrate his Sukkoth holiday together with teachers and children who were the very target of the ban.

"Don't allow it!" was Rav Zorach's reaction as a man deeply involved in Jerusalem education. "And if you can't prevent it, you must run away from there. In any case, you are obligated by halacha to protest."

Reb Yoel finished his ablutions quickly and sped back home. As he approached he saw that half the huge school *sukka* had already been erected, with his wall as its retaining side. Boys and girls were busily arranging *sechach* covering. His zeal filled him with courage and impetus and he shouted a bitter shout with all his might, "Here in Jerusalem?! Here in Jerusalem?!" The passersby stopped at his terrifying cries, but the teachers commanded their pupils to attack the old man and silence his shouting. Obediently, the boys surrounded him in an instant, like a swarm of bees, and trampled the elderly Reb Yoel to the ground, leaving him bleeding and stunned. Then they returned to their happy labors as if nothing had happened.

Helpful, concerned neighbors rushed to the old man's aid and brought him, bleeding and wounded, to the hospital. Still stunned by the rapid events, the old zealot exclaimed over and over, "Here in Jerusalem?! Oy! Oy! Here in Jerusalem?!"

The sun set; the stars came out. Throngs of Jews filled the synagogues for the holiday prayers. But in the Batey Machseh *shul* not far from Mount Zion, the people sat and waited for their neighbor, Rav Chayim Sonnenfeld, to appear. That great man, who was later to be crowned Rav of the Holy City, had taken advantage of the pause between *mincha* and *ma'ariv* to go together with Reb Yaakov Blumenthal to visit Reb Yoel Erhentreu and help alleviate the pain he had suffered in his zealous stand for the cause of pure education in Jerusalem.

Rumor had it that the great men of Jerusalem were streaming to the old man's bedside at the command of the Brisker Rav, to pay their respects and wish him a speedy recovery.

And indeed, during Chol Hamoed, Reb Yoel, who was still bedridden, was visited by the élite of Jerusalem society, among them the elderly Maggid of Vilkomir. Reb Yoel became emotional, begging the sage's forgiveness for having inconvenienced him. He then asked him candidly, "Tell me, was my protest sufficient? Did I fulfill what was incumbent on me in the way of protest?"

The old Maggid heaved a heavy sigh and answered, "Who knows? Who knows if we fulfill our obligations? Who knows if more isn't demanded?"

Eyewitnesses reported that after that incident, whenever Reb Yoel went to visit the Brisker Rav, the Rav would offer him a seat — a rare honor indeed!

Many years after that horrible episode, one chilling fact was put on record.

In the year 5684, six years after Reb Yoel's death, Zionist fanatics coldbloodedly murdered the saintly religious activist, Reb Yaakov Yisrael Dehaan. At the funeral, one of the mourners stood up and testified that the hand that had pulled the trigger to release the deadly bullet that killed Reb Yaakov Yisrael as he was returning home from *ma'ariv* was the identical hand that had been first raised in bloody violence against old Reb Yoel Ehrentreu many years before in the *sukka* incident.

The Personality That Was Reb Yoel

As a matter of fact, the Brisker Rav *did* offer Reb Yoel a chair, but anyone who was familiar with Reb Yoel knew well enough that he did not seek that chair. Had he sought it and what it stood for, he and his household would not have lived in such dire poverty.

His former mentor, the Rav of Pressburg, author of *Sheivet Sofer* and president of the Kolel Shomray Ha-Chomoth, once proposed Reb Yoel for the position of treasurer of the Kolel's funds, which entailed their just allocation.

Such a coveted position could have solved all of Reb Yoel's financial problems, for it was a job that paid well, but Reb Yoel fled this job and the honor that went along with it. He shied away from all titles.

Reb Yoel sent an apologetic letter of refusal to his former *rebbi,* in which he wrote,

"Forgive me, honored rabbi, that I am unable this time to comply with your holy will and to accept this honored position upon my shoulders. I fear for my soul, if I were to approach a community treasury and maintain its accounts of incoming and outgoing funds, debits, credits, and deficits. All the more so am I wary of apportioning charity funds, of determining who is worthy of a larger or a smaller share — for fear of erring in the allocation of communal funds by even a single coin. For then I would have to render account before my Maker, the God of

Israel. So I beg you to free me of these garments of priesthood which are too big for me. And my thanks are yours in advance."

Reb Yoel did not depend on the letter alone. He also went down to the Kothel haMaaravi to pour out his heart to the Blessed One, asking that He soften the determination of the Pressburg Rav and make him retract his offer; he abandoned the suggestion. Thus was Reb Yoel 'saved' from a public position that would have paid him handsomely, suffering instead in his impoverished state until his last day.

Rabbi Dr. Yaakov Yisrael deHaan

The Bookbinder's Marriage

BEING OFFERED a seat by Rav Yehoshua Leib Diskin was an almost unheard-of and cherished honor in the eyes of Jerusalem Jewry. Anyone thus honored by the Brisker Rav likewise acquired the respect of the local people. Jerusalem's Jews held the Brisker Rav in their highest esteem; they regarded him with an exalted love from the day he set foot in their city. And even the slightest look, the merest glance from his holy eyes, set the trend for the whole city.

Jerusalem's Jews were one big family in those days. The community was prodigious in quality, but tiny in quantity. Hate and jealousy did not even exist. All were equally poor, equally immersed in Torah study and the pursuit of mitzvoth, young as well as old. Each person was subservient to his neighbor and all subservient to the Torah-giants who were their leaders.

They celebrated their *smachoth* together, whether *brith,* bar mitzva, or marriage. All were invited to participate, and all rejoiced equally with a new soul, or at a marriage — on Friday afternoons in most cases — which took place in the combined homes of adjacent neighbors.

The Jerusalem Jews did not come to indulge themselves in fat dinners — they were not offered any to begin with. Each wedding had a standard menu.

There was, however, one wedding that proved to be an exception, and it became the talk of the town: Manish the bookbinder's wedding.

128

Why was this wedding so unusual? Who was Manish the bookbinder?

It all started with the slight hint that Rav Yehoshua Leib Diskin dropped to the *gabbai* of the Kerem *shul*, Reb Zimmel, implying that participation in the bookbinder's wedding was singularly important.

"Well," they said, "if Reb Zimmel, a man so close to the Brisker Rav, says that the Rav hinted thus, then there is no reason to doubt his words," decided the disciples of the Brisker Rav. Reb Zimmel was an honest man who lived by the sweat of his brow even while dedicating most of his days to Torah and prayer. His four sons-in-law, choice young scholars in Jerusalem yeshivos, were all supported by him.

Manish's wedding took place in the Kerem section of Jerusalem where his elderly parents lived — his father long since bedridden with disease, and his mother crippled by the whip of a Turkish porter on the very day she set foot on holy soil. It was celebrated on one of the shorter Friday afternoons in Teveth and, although the weather itself was warm and pleasant, the roads were muddy. This did not deter people from attending, however, and wagonload after wagonload arrived from the Old City to the neighborhood outside the walls, spewing forth an enormous crowd of people. Among these were the majority of Jerusalem's elite. Rav Yosef Chayim Sonnenfeld, the *mesader kidushin,* was accompanied by his son, Reb Avraham Aharon. Reb Yissachar Dov Zwebner, son of Rav Avraham Shag, with his wife, were honored with leading the bridal couple to the *chuppa.* Rav Zevulun Charlap of the Brisker Rav's *beith din* was present, as were Rav Zorach Braverman, Rav Nota Tzvi Weiss, the famous *maggid*, Rav Zalman B'horan and his brothers Rav David, Rav Shalom Pester, and many others.

The carriage bearing the *kalla,* Zlata, the niece of Reb Moshe Shochet Frankenthal, who was one of the chief disciples of the Brisker Rav, arrived. The same carriage brought the Brisker rebbetzin, Rav Shmuel Salant's respected wife, the wife of the famed Rav Shneyer Zalman of Lublin, Mattel Biderman, wife of Reb Davidl, and Rebbetzin Sherel Sonnenfeld. Other worthy women also appeared, loaded down with heavy baskets full of jars of herring pickled especially for the wedding feast and decorated with lemon slices and bay leaves, and with cakes, pastries, and bagels that had shared the oven with Shaboss *challoth.* The good women also brought a large barrel of aged wine that had been collectively donated by families in the Old City, and pillowcases full of sunflower seeds, chick peas, and nuts.

The square in front of the synagogue filled and the crowd expanded tidally from minute to minute into a sea of *shtreimels,* crowding up front as if each were the *chathan*'s closest relative. As the sun began its descent from the treetops, Reb Zimmel hurried the last minute preparations. A gold and silver embroidered *chuppa* was lifted over the heads of the *chathan* and his attendants. The *kalla* was led under it. Then Rav Chayim Sonnenfeld began the ceremony.

Why did the Brisker Rav see fit to invite — almost summon — Jerusalem's elite to this wedding of a simple bookbinder of nineteen? Why did he deem it necessary to assemble these men and women on the shortest of Fridays in the midst of their hurried Shabbath preparations?

No one knew. A small group of people, however, were fortunate enough, that Shabbath evening after *ma'ariv,* to hear Reb Avraham Aharon Sonnenfeld explain his father's motive.

130

The Only Son of Old Age

"It BEGAN ON the twenty-first of Iyar in the year 5633 — thirty years ago," began Reb Avraham Aharon. "That was when my father arrived in Jerusalem, accompanying his *rebbi*, the famous Rav Avraham Shag of Kaubersdorf. My father was only twenty-four years old then and the Jewish community was in the beginning of its development. The Batey Machseh section, which had been completed a short while before, was the only Jewish neighborhood at the time outside of some scattered Jewish homes built among Arab dwellers. Any Jew who left his homeland in Europe in order to settle in Jerusalem could expect only hardship and suffering before he found a safe haven he could call home.

"The good people of Kaubersdorf were well aware of this problem and had made provisions beforehand for their esteemed Rav. When he arrived in Jerusalem there was a small apartment waiting for him in Batey Machseh. Not so my father, who was so humble and retiring that no one even knew that he intended to go to Jerusalem together with his *rebbi* until he set foot on ship's deck. Since no living quarters had been prepared for him, he was forced to spend several nights under the cover of the Jerusalem sky. My mother joked about her plight then, saying that she had expected to live in Batey Machseh — the Houses of Shelter — and found that she had neither a house nor a shelter. Rav Avraham

131

Shag was deeply distressed about the situation but there was nothing that he could do.

"Rav Avraham Shag had a neighbor who was also distressed by the fact that the young man and his wife had no roof over their heads. Reb Noach Yudel, originally from Dvinsk, and a carpenter by profession, took the problem to heart and decided to do something about it. This Reb Yudel was no simple man. Throughout the many years that he had lived in Jerusalem he had been active in communal affairs. He had, in addition, built a *shtender* for the renowned Rav Nachum Levi of Sadik on which that Rav had studied throughout the years. He had designed and executed the new *bima* in the large Churva *shul* and he had crafted the huge carved doors of the Misgav Ladach Hospital.

"The name he made for himself as a craftsman was surpassed only by the good name he acquired for his integrity and good heart. Reb Yudel plied his trade for four hours daily, dedicating the remainder of the day to study and prayer. He kept his mouth closed, fleeing from any hint of forbidden speech. His lips formed only holy words; going and coming from his workshop, they moved constantly in prayer and study.

"Reb Yudel divined the hidden treasure in Rav Avraham's modest disciple. Seeing that the young man had no place to call home and no money to enable him to acquire such a place, he resolved to do something about the situation. Reb Yudel was the kind of man who, having once decided that something must be done, does not rest until that thing is done. Within three days he found a small flat in an Arab building, paid two months' rent in advance and furnished the humble abode with a table and chairs of his own making. It was then all ready for my father to inhabit it, which the young man and his wife gratefully did.

"Rav Avraham Shag, learning of Reb Yudel's dedicated efforts on behalf of his disciple, went to the carpenter to thank him personally and to let him know something about the object of his kindness. 'You have prepared a home for a great light which will soon illuminate the skies of the Holy Land. Surely this great merit will stand you in good stead for the rest of your life,' Rav Avraham told the carpenter as he stood on the threshold of his neighbor's house.

"Rav Avraham turned to go, but the carpenter barred his way, and burst into tears. 'Rebbi, if I indeed performed an act of merit, then I did so without realizing the true value of your disciple and without expecting gain of any kind. Therefore, for the sake of this mitzva, I beg of you, please bless me with children.'

"Reb Yudel tried to hold back his torrent of tears as he provided some background to his tragedy. 'I have been married for twenty years already, *rebbi*.' He added that a celebrated Viennese doctor had recently visited Jerusalem and had told the couple that there was no hope for them. Reb Yudel's wife was in the next room, and Rav Avraham could hear her sobs as her husband presented his request.

"The *tzaddik* from Kaubersdorf thought for a short while, his face aglow and his eyes assuming a strange cast. Then he suddenly promised Reb Yudel that he and his wife would be truly be blessed with a son in the course of the coming year.

"The year had not yet completed its cycle when his blessing was realized and the middle-aged couple celebrated their newborn son. His *brith* was celebrated on *erev* Pesach of the year 5634 in the Batey Machseh synagogue.

Rav Avraham Shag was honored as *sandak* and my
father was the *mohel*. The boy born twenty-one years
after Reb Yudel's marriage was named Manish, after
his grandfather, Reb Manish Aidels, who had belonged
to the inner circle of the Vilna Gaon's disciples. A huge
feast celebrated the occasion, in which all the important
people of Jerusalem participated and, true to his character, Reb Yudel set aside one table on the eastern wall
and had it heaped lavishly with good food for all the
poor people of the city.

"Reb Yudel and his wife had hoped to entrust the
boy to Rav Avraham's tutelage but that great man departed this world when Manish was a child of not yet
three. And strangely enough, Reb Yudel was forewarned
of the *tzaddik's* death.

"It happened on a Friday evening, on the 28th of Adar
5636, after Reb Yudel had just finished his Shabbath meal.
He fully intended to go to Rav Meir Auerbach's home.
for that Rav from Kalish, famed author of *Imray Bina*,
customarily expounded on Torah thoughts and *mussar*
ideas from the weekly portion before a huge crowd. Reb
Yudel finished *birchath ha-mazon* and was on the verge
of leaving when he was overtaken by a heavy slumber.
In this deep sleep he dreamed he saw one of the ancient
and cherished Torah scrolls in the ark of the Batey
Machseh *shul* burning, God forbid. He awoke in a fright.
But the dreadful dream did not deter him from rushing
to the home of the Kalisher Rav.

"Reb Yudel had not missed the lecture. When it was
over, and the people began to return to their respective
homes, Reb Yudel approached the Rav, and feelingly
repeated his frightening dream. The Rav listened in fear,
and then told Reb Yudel how to observe the halachah
about fasting for a bad dream on Shabbath.

"By the following morning the news was all over the city: Rav Avraham Shag had been summoned to the heavenly realms. The matter was discussed at the Rav of Kalish's Shabbath table that day. One of his disciples remarked how strange it was that an event of such moment to the Jewish community should have been revealed beforehand to a mere carpenter. But the Rav answered shortly, 'Simple wooden vessels do not absorb *tum'a.*'

"A year passed and Manish began *cheider*. His father borrowed the *tallith* that had belonged to Rav Avraham Shag for the momentous occasion and, wrapped up in that holy garment, the boy was brought to commence his Torah education at the Etz Chayim *cheider*.

"The lad excelled and was promoted from class to class with a rapidity that astounded his teachers. The years sped by, years full of *nachath* for the elderly parents. On one occasion Reb Yudel met Rav Eliezer Dan Ralbag on the street and the latter related in glowing terms that he had tested the boy's knowledge just that week and Manish had excelled in understanding and erudition. On the next day Rav Davidl Biderman stopped the carpenter in the marketplace and also spoke highly about the boy's piety in prayer and general enthusiasm for mitzvoth.

"Although his parents pinned great hopes upon their only son, Manish didn't succeed in fulfilling them all. Before he became seventeen Manish's father became paralyzed and bedridden. His crippled mother likewise soon took to her bed. There was no choice but for Manish to seek some way to support the family and, knowing that his parents' lives were at stake, he did not hesitate long. Within a month he had learned bookbinding, rented a tiny shop on Jews' Street, and hung out his shingle.

"He worked diligently but earned sparingly. No wonder,

for he spent most of his days studying; his profession was only incidental. He did not leave his learning partners, never missing a *shi'ur* in the yeshiva or a session with his close friend Yeshaya Cheshin, his learning partner of many years' standing.

The Book Critic

"THE STORE HAD BEEN OPEN for business for about two weeks when the Brisker Rav happened to pass by, accompanied by a train of disciples. Noticing the modest new shop, he asked his disciples about it and was informed by Reb Yitzchak Shlomo Blau, who knew about the young Manish who had been forced to turn his hand to a livelihood. To the great surprise of all his *talmidim*, the Rav stepped into the tiny shop. He found Manish in the midst of his work. When the young lad looked up and saw the Brisker Rav standing before him in the flesh, in his own shop, he nearly fainted. His tools fell out of his trembling hands, his voice stuck momentarily in his throat. Then he arose and said in full humility, 'Rebbi... I have opened a bookbinding store here... p-please bless me.'

"The Brisker Rav stretched out his hand to the lad, 'My son, beware of taking in secular books by "progressive" and atheistic writers. If you are careful, the labor of your hands will be blessed.' His *talmidim* heard his words and quickly answered, '*Vihi noam* — May the pleasure of HaShem be upon us and the labor of our hands...'

"The Rav and his entourage left the store and continued on their way, leaving Manish stunned by the surprise visit of the great man to his tiny shop. And little wonder! Even great men proudly boasted when the Brisker Rav spoke only one or two words to them, while Manish could claim a personal visit!

" 'Who am I and what am I that I have merited this?' he murmured to himself. That was the end of work for Manish that day. Instead he spent the remainder in repentance and prayer hoping that Heaven would assist him in heeding the Rav's exhortation. And from that day on, when Manish opened his shop in the morning he would stop at the mezuza on the doorpost and offer a short prayer, '*Ribono shel olam*, this humble being prostrates itself before You in a plea. Don't let me, God forbid, stumble in my work and unknowingly transgress the ban on binding a suspicious book...' Only then would he proceed to his daily work, ignoring the tiny tears that invariably formed in his eyes.

"Days passed and the Rav's visit, which had been the talk of all Jerusalem, was forgotten. Manish meanwhile had acquired a name as being an accomplished tradesman. The Jews of Jerusalem put their trust in his craftsmanship and he did not lack business.

" 'It is not an unattainable ideal,' Reb Leibush Weber would say, pointing to Manish as his perfect example, 'to fulfill the words of the *Mesilath Yesharim* that "one can be a true *chassid* even if circumstances force him to perform simple labor." '

"Seated at his workbench, sewing, pasting, aligning pages and being thoroughly involved in his work, Manish could be heard murmuring a half-silent prayer, 'My Father in heaven, I, Manish the son of Miriam Dvora, beseech you to save me from having a forbidden book find its way to my shop... Oh, *Ribono shel olam*, help me fulfill what is written in Your Torah, "How shall a youth justify his path to persevere in Your commands." '

"The truth was that Manish would not have recognized

a forbidden book if he had held one between his hands. He knew about Torah, *Nevi'im* and *Kethuvim*. He knew about *Shass* and *poskim*. But what kind of books did heretics write? He could not fathom. He had heard denunciations, upon the several occasions when *mussar* lecturers had visited the yeshiva, of *'bichelach'* and newspapers. He had seen these denunciations reinforced in sacred *seforim*. But that a questionable book should actually find its way into the holy city of Jerusalem — that was something he could not even imagine possible!

"No wonder then, that worry gnawed inside him. Who knows, he fretted, if I have not at some time inadvertently bound forbidden books without even being aware of it? He had even heard his teacher, Rav Eliezer Dan Ralbag, reveal that there were some Jews sporting long beards and worthy deeds who had been ensnared by progressiveness. Maybe, thought Manish, I would be better off finding some different occupation altogether, something that is free from pitfalls and consequently not as dangerous.

"It happened once, during the *'bein ha-metzarim'* period, the three-week interval between the two fast days commemorating the destruction of the *beith ha-mikdash*, that Manish was subjected to temptation in the very area he feared. He used to close his shop before noon during those introspective days in order to join the worshipers at the Mechavnim *shul* in reciting the *tikkun chatzoth* in the daytime. Just as he was locking up one day, an honored client entered. It was the *tzaddik* Rav Meshel Gelbstein, who had come to bind a *'Chidushay HaRim,'* which had just been sent to him from Warsaw where it had been published.

"Manish took this opportune moment to bare his problem to the saintly man. Rav Meshel heard the youth's conflict and sighed, 'You have touched upon a serious problem, my son, one which must really be posed to a qualified rabbi. You cannot rely on your own judgment in this matter; it is like playing with fire.'

"At that moment they heard the *shamash* of the Chevra Kadisha announcing the death of Rav Mordechai Eliezer Weber, the zealous Rav of Oda. Rav Meshel ran outside and prodded the bookbinder to follow suit. 'A great man has left us. All work must cease.' Rav Meshel proceeded to the funeral, followed by Manish. On their way they met Rav Akiva Yosef Schlesinger, author of *'Lev HaIvri,'* and Rav Meshel remembered Manish's question. He grabbed the youth's hand and led him to Rav Akiva Yosef, saying, 'Here is your qualified rabbi. He will be able to direct you in your work.'

"Rav Meshel then explained the young bookbinder's dilemma to Rav Akiva Yosef and, vouching for the young tradesman, begged him to direct the youth. Rav Akiva Yosef thought about it for a short while and then agreed. Manish felt deeply relieved and would have danced for joy had he not been at a funeral, for a heavy burden had been rolled off his heart.

"From that day on Manish did not bind any book before it had gone through the critical hands of Rav Akiva Yosef. There was one drawback, however. Since his new critic tended to judge books rather harshly, Manish's business was diminished by half. Who, in the Jerusalem of then, had the money to spend on binding books anyway, if not for progressive men like Pines, Yellin, and their ilk, the representatives of Chovevey Zion. They could afford to bind their books lavishly, too, in leather and cloth with gold letters — work that they paid generously for.

"Manish's circumstances grew increasingly difficult. After the monthly allotment he gave his parents, he barely had a few coins left to live on himself. For a long period all Manish ate was dark bread with a little sesame oil that he bought from the Arabs. His neighbors in the Kerem section testified that not a drop of milk entered his lips for months at a time. But nothing could allay his happiness in having found, through God's kind help, a patron who supervised his work and kept him from stumbling through ignorance into error."

At this point Reb Avraham Aharon's avid listeners interrupted his story. "All right, so Manish is a singularly Godfearing young man. But all he is, in the end, is a mere bookbinder. How did he become the husband of the famous Reb Moshe Frankenthal's niece, a *tzaddeikess* in her own right, famed throughout the city for her character and good deeds? Is there a dearth of *talmidey chachamim* that this particular young man was chosen as her partner?"

Reb Avraham heard their comments but did not react He merely continued the thread of his story.

"One day, as Manish was working at his books, a Yemeni Jew stopped in front of the store and began unloading a heavily-laden donkey. He untied bundle after bundle of books and handed five gold coins to Manish. Such a sum was enough to support an entire family for a whole month! What's more, he promised the young bookbinder, in the name of his employer, that if the books were bound well he would receive further payment.

"Manish was at a loss. Indeed the fat down payment and the huge array of books seemed very suspicious to him, and he wanted to stop the Jew from unloading the bundles then and there. But he was loathe to bother a worker who had labored so much already simply on the chance that these books were questionable. Fortunately, at that moment, Reb Moshe Frankenthal happened to pass

141

by and Manish pounced on him happily and dragged him inside. Reb Moshe let himself be led by the insistent book-binder. He took one of the books into his hands and it fell open to the title page: *'Children of My Spirit,* by Michel Pines,' it read. Reb Moshe, thoroughly agitated, threw the book away: It was heretical through and through. Manish didn't need to be told anything more explicit than that; he immediately told the Yemeni Jew to take his mer-chandise back where it came from. Returning the five gold pieces, and adding a few coins for the man's labors, he began to reload the donkey, and then accompanied the man a few steps despite his protests.

" 'But my employer is a Jew with a long beard. He wears a long rabbinical coat. What could be wrong with these books?' the Yemeni wondered. But Manish per-sisted and sent the man on his way.

"Reb Moshe was deeply impressed by the youth's righteousness and at the wellspring of strength inside him that enabled him to withstand such temptation in his circumstances of poverty. He decided then and there to have the boy marry his renowned and excellent niece and spoke to the girl's father that very day. Reb Yaakov Orenstein took his brother-in-law's word as to the book-binder's suitability and the match was confirmed."

It was no idle rumor, the disciples of the Brisker Rav finally agreed, when Reb Zimmel said that the great Rav had hinted at the importance of participating in this wedding. His disciples now understood as well why the wedding had been graced by the two-hour-long dancing of three Jerusalem celebrities: Rav Eliezer Dan Ralbag, Reb Yaakov Blumenthal and Reb Tuvya Goldberger. Who could hear their ecstatic singing of *"Yibaneh —* let the *beith hamikdash* be rebuilt and the city of Zion filled" — without joining in fervently?

The Afikomon Gift

JERUSALEM'S JEWS thrilled to carry out the Brisker Rav's slightest hint of a wish. They treasured his every holy movement, exulted at the hope of a blessing from his holy lips. One who was fortunate enough to actually receive his benediction was considered a lucky man, for hadn't the Jews of Jerusalem seen, with their own eyes, how the *tzaddik* decreed and God fulfilled?

Sara, daughter of Rav Akiva Yosef Schlesinger, longed for such a blessing for her nine-year-old son. She constantly prodded her husband, David, to take their little Zalmanke in to Rav Yehoshua Leib Diskin for a *bracha* that the boy grow up to be a pious Jew. Each time David would put her off.

"I can't do it," he argued. "One doesn't go in to the Brisker Rav just like that and ask for a *bracha.* It may seem a simple thing to a woman, but it just isn't done! Even great men hesitate to enter his chamber, and tremble in fear before his holy presence. What do you want from me, a mere young man?"

David went further and told his wife about the letter that the Brisker Rav had just received from one of the leaders of the generation, the renowned Rav Yosef Dov Ber Soloveitchik, author of *Beith Haleivi* and present Rav of Brisk. This great person had written, "My hands have been trembling for two weeks since I began writing this letter to the great Rav Yehoshua Leib Diskin."

143

"And if our leaders approach the Brisker Rav with such trepidation, what should I say?" he concluded.

Sara heard all of his explanations and his hesitations, but did not change her mind. On the contrary, the more he exalted the figure of the Rav, the greater grew her desire to have her son blessed by him. Yet the harder she persisted, the firmer grew his refusal. "I am too much awed by him," he would reply.

As the holiday of Pesach approached, Sara began to renew her request with fresh fervor, "You are among the top ten disciples of the Rav. You were chosen to found his Yeshiva Ohel Moshe. Is it so hard for you to enter and ask him to bless your child?"

David did not give in.

When this righteous woman saw that her tears did not move him, she devised a different plan. On *erev*-Pesach she called her Zalmanke to her and coached him in his role. At the *seider* table, he was to snatch away the *afikomon*. Then, later, he was to refuse to return it until his father agreed to take him in to the Rav for a blessing

Zalmanke was both naive and cunning. His quick hands stole the coveted *afikomon* while his father was retelling the epic redemption from Egypt. When the time came to eat the *afikoman,* David noticed that it was gone — according to custom. He had no idea, however, that this time he would have to pay dearly to redeem it.

"I'll buy you a copy of *Nefesh HaChayim*," he offered in exchange for the matza.

Zalmanke was not to be bought off so easily.

"I'll buy you a *Peney Yehoshua*," David suggested.

He refused. Prize after prize was dangled before him, but Zalmanke accepted none of his father's offers, wanting only what his mother maintained was rightfully his — a blessing from the Brisker Rav. Sara sat facing him across the *seider* table and smiled to Zalmanke, encouraging him not to give in until he extracted the promise from his father.

It was getting late, and David clearly saw that he had no choice but to give in to the boy. Unable to promise, he consented to try with all his might. Zalmanke, who could not expect more than that, relinquished the *afikomon* with a beaming face.

When the first day of Chol Hamoed Pesach arrived, Zalmanke reminded his father of the promise. There was no way out, and so, as soon as David returned from *musaf,* he announced to his happy household that he would take Zalmanke — finally — to the Brisker Rav. Sara's heart pounded with joy. Her lips murmured a prayer that this hour would be favorable, an opportune time for the *bracha* to flow without interference from the *tzaddik* to the boy.

David took the dancing little boy by his hand, and they went together toward the Rav's house. The boy's face expressed boundless joy. One minute more and then another minute and then . . . then the great Brisker Rav would place his saintly hands upon Zalmanke's head and would bless him. . . finally!

They reached the house and even approached the Rav's study. David took a peek through the crack to see in what setting he would find the Rav. His eyes took in the Rav's holiday garb and the holy face that was illuminated with majesty. He was seated on his chair, deeply immersed in thought. The room was completely quiet. To his left and right were famous *rabbanim* of the city: Rav Yosef Chayim Sonnenfeld, Rav Hirsh Michel Shapira, Rav Yeshaya Orenstein and his son Rav Yaakov, Rav Naftali Hertz Haleivi of Jaffa and and Rav Eliezer Dan Ralbag — all were sitting in meditation and trepidation without moving a limb. All eyes were turned toward the central figure of the Rav which glowed with holiness and whose spirit transcended their mortal surroundings.

David took this all in with a brief glance and shied back quickly. This was surely not the time to open the door and enter! His heart beat wildly and taking his son's hand he stepped further back, prepared to go home empty-handed with the disappointed Zalmanke. But at this point the boy burst into tears.

The rebbetzin, hearing the youthful weeping, hurried to see what caused it. She recognized the boy and offered him almonds and sweet wine to still his cries, but he continued sobbing bitterly. "What do you want, Zalmanke?" she asked him with motherly concern. "Tell me and I'll give it to you." But Zalmanke, unable to speak because of his choking sobs, did not answer.

"Where is your father?" she asked him. When he pointed to the outer room, she went to ask David why the child was weeping so intensely.

"He wants a *bracha* from the Rav," the father answered truthfully.

"Well, well," she replied good-naturedly, "if he has shed such a multitude of tears for it, he surely deserves one. I myself will take him inside to the Rav." Within seconds the two figures had entered the room. The Rav had just shaken off his state of semi-trance and he now listened to his wife's plea. He then raised his palms, placed them upon the small head of the boy, and blessed him saying,

"Let it be God's Will that you be *'an ehrlicher Yid,'* a true Jew."

The boy himself joined in the *Amein* that everyone heartily pronounced. And David, who had meanwhile gone to his son's side, managed to say that one word too before a torrent of tears gushed down his face.

Meanwhile Sara stood expectantly by her window. Her eager eyes impatiently scoured the street for some sign of the returning heroes. Suddenly she saw the flying figure of Zalmanke catapulting toward home. She ran out to catch her happy offspring in joyful arms with a prayer of thanks on her lips that God had fulfilled her request.

It is interesting to note that the very window upon whose sill she leaned and waited so eagerly, the window of Rav Akiva Yosef Schlesinger's home, faced the Kothel haMaaravi. The single pane of glass had been bathed with numerous prayers and tears. Liba, the wife of Rav Akiva Yosef and daughter of Rav Hillel of Kolomya, used to stand at this very window and pour out her prayers to the One Who had caused His Name to dwell in the holy place that she could clearly see. Her prayers revolved around one theme — that the coming generations, fruit of her womb, would be righteous men, men of integrity, *tzaddikim*.

Rebbetzin Liba offered another *tefilla* on Thursdays from the same window. She would pray that the objects of value that she still owned would fetch a good price at the pawnshop so that she would have the half a napoleon needed to cover her Shabbath expenses. She begged God to invest her with grace in the eyes of the dealer so that he would give her the needed coin. . . .

And they say that Liba's prayers were almost always answered.

Zalmanke Returns Barefoot from Chevron

"AN EHRLICHER YID" was the *bracha* that the Brisker Rav bestowed upon little Zalmanke, son of Reb David, and that is what he became. From that momentous day until his death, Zalman was enveloped with an aura of holiness, abstinence, and purity. All of his deeds were solely for God's sake.

One Chol Hamoed Sukkoth found the entire city in a state of confusion bordering on hysteria. Rav Hirsh Michel Shapira, one of the beloved Jews of the city, had suffered a serious fainting spell, some kind of stroke. The city reverberated with prayers for his quick recovery. When he awoke from his prolonged faint and regained consciousness, his family wished to remove him from the *sukka* to the safety and comfort of his home. Although he resisted with his last ounce of strength, he was easily overpowered by his well-intentioned family who carried him into his house, in accordance with the halachic decision of the Brisker Rav.

When he was safely deposited inside, the members of his family asked him why he had fought them so vigorously.

"I thought that was my last hour. I didn't want to willingly desert the dear mitzva of *sukka* at that crucial time," he explained.

Even within the confines of his home, however, Rav Hirch Michel's condition was critical. Yerushalmim ran to the Kothel haMaaravi to pray for his speedy recovery;

The building over the cave of the Machpeila

The main entrance to the cave of Machpeila

others sped to the graves of *tzaddikim* on Har haZeithim to beg them to intervene for him in heavenly circles; still others went to inform the Brisker Rav and to join him in prayer.

In the midst of this confusion, it was discovered that fourteen-year-old Zalmanke had disappeared. Zalman's mother was the only one who was not worried. "He is surely hiding in some *shul* and saying *Tehilim* for Rav Hirsh Michel," she reassured her worried husband.

Day waned: night swept over the city. Still no Zalman. Reb David suddenly thought of looking for Zalman's *lulav* and *ethrog*. They were gone. Evidently Zalman had intended on staying wherever he was until the following morning. *But where can the boy have gone?* his father wondered.

All that night David worried, but the next morning Zalmanke appeared with another boy. He was carrying his *lulav* and *ethrog* in his right hand, and in his left, a pair of shoes. The boy walked in barefoot.

"Where have you been, Zalmanke? And why are you barefoot?" his family rained questions upon the boy's head.

All the answers revolved around Rav Hirsh Michel's sudden fainting spell. As Zalmanke's traveling companion explained to the family, the boy had been present when the *tzaddik* took ill. All shaken up by it, he had run home to grab his *lulav* and *ethrog* and had then gone to his friend. The friend had hired a donkey and they had set off for Chevron to *daven* at the graves of our forefathers at the Me'arath haMachpeila.

The two boys had spent the entire night in *tefilla,* which they culminated with a dip in the *mikveh* of the kabbalist, Rav Eliyahu Mani, and with *vathikin* prayers. Then they had headed homeward.

When they were well on their way, the friend remarked that Zalman's shoes looked strange. "You must have switched shoes with someone else at the *mikveh,"* he told him. Zalman quickly took off the offending shoes. "It amounts to robbery," he said, "to wear someone else's shoes. Let us return to Chevron so that I can seek out the owner of the strange shoes." But his friend refused. "It would take too much time to track down the owner. Besides, your parents are probably worried enough about you as it is." Zalman was forced to agree, but traveled the entire way back to Jerusalem barefoot.

When David heard the story of the shoes, he grew angry. "You should have returned to Chevron right away to seek the owner of the shoes. You do not let a mitzva slip out of your hands at an opportune moment."

And so, that very day, Zalman returned to Chevron to seek the owner of the shoes. It was not in vain that Yerushalmim pointed to Zalman as a personification of the Brisker Rav's blessing. As for Zalmanke, the true Jew, his prayer may have been the one that attained another year of life for Rav Hirsh Michel.

The Copper Key

RAV HIRSH MICHEL passed away on the twelfth of Elul, 5666, and the entire Batey Machseh turned out for the funeral. The streets were black with crowds of men, women, and children streaming toward the Mount of Olives; all stores were shut; all work was stopped. The city mourned its irreplaceable loss. The presence of this beloved *tzaddik* would grace the city no more.

The *shamash* of the Chevra Kadisha claimed the attention of the mourners by announcing in his resonant voice, "Any person who sends his children to secular schools shall not venture near the deceased." The square filled up with more people from one minute to the next and the air reverberated with the youthful voices of *cheider* boys chanting *Yosheiv Beseither Elyon* verse by verse.

The list of eulogizers was impressive and included the cream of Jerusalem's scholars. Heading the list was Rav Yosef Chayim Sonnenfeld; second was Rav Yitzchak Vinograd. The atmosphere was taut with emotion. The crowd wept silently and even the heavens shed teardrops from their grey, overcast heights. To heighten the tension, word of a strange happening swept the crowd. It was said that the deceased had been found with a copper key in his hand. No one knew where this key was from, what door it unlocked, or what it signified.

The Chevra Kadisha sent someone to ask the rebbetzin if she knew what key it was, but she had not the slightest idea. Neither did Rav Ben-Zion, the son of the deceased. He had never seen the key before, and had not even known of its existence.

One man suddenly recalled a similar occurrence. Three years before, when the head of the Yeshivath Beith-El Chassidim, Chacham Sasson Persaido, author of *Shemen Sasson* and *Pethach Enayim,* had departed this world he had also been found with a key similar to this one...

This reminiscence evoked yet another. The famous *shotheik* — the silent one — Rav Baruch Yosef Zisserman, known by this title for the infrequency with which his voice was heard, came forward with a recollection of his childhood. He remembered that when the renowned Rav Nachum Levi of Sadik had passed away, such a copper key had been found on the table in his study. Then, as now, no one had been able to identify the key. Since none of these stories shed any light on the present mystery, the funeral proceeded through the eulogies and ended with the final trek to the burial grounds. During the next three days the strange incident was all but forgotten.

Rav Shmuel Salant, Rav of Jerusalem, was at this time an old, old man of ninety. He had served his community faithfully some seventy of those years, but now rarely took part in communal affairs or family events. His failing sight and his waning strength prevented him from even venturing out of his home. Instead, he had a *minyan* of young men from Yeshiva Etz Chayim come to his home to *daven* on weekdays, Shabbath, and Yom Tov.

On the eighteenth day of Elul, after *shacharith,* Rav Shmuel called his faithful attendant, Reb Eliyahu Mordechai Eisenstein, to him and asked if he were willing to accompany him on a condolence visit to the home of the departed Reb Hirsh Michel. The mere suggestion threw Reb Eliyahu into a near fit, for the Rav's proposal was unrealistic. "The Rav does not even take a step inside his own home unaided. How can you expect to reach Batey Machseh?" he asked in consternation. At first, he tried to divert the elderly Rav's attention, but that didn't work. He then recruited the rest of the family to help convince Rav Shmuel that the idea was unsound, that it even presented a physical danger to his life. Rav Shmuel did not waver. He energetically donned his black silk robe, the one reserved from the times he had sat on his *beith din*. Leaning his right arm on Reb Eliyahu's shoulder and his left arm on the shoulder of Reb Yoshe Rivlin, secretary of Va'ad haKlali, he prepared to go.

At the last moment, Reb Yosef Binyamin Shimanowitz, the *shochet,* still essayed to stop him. This plan, he argued, conflicted with the Torah edict that obligated a man to guard his own life. Rav Shmuel did not reply directly. He merely sighed and exclaimed woefully, "Oy! Oy! Holy Rav Hirsh Michel is with us no longer!"

The members of his household saw now that further argument would be superfluous. Nothing in the world would deter the Rav from paying his intended condolence visit, and so they let him leave the house.

After he had gone a few steps, a chair was quickly brought by one of the young men of the Etz Chayim yeshiva. In a flash the Rav was seated upon it and carried royally to his destination. It was a grand spectacle. And anyone who saw the famous Rav thus transported through the streets, especially after he had not made a public appearance for years, felt obligated to follow behind. Once again, Rav Hirsh Michel's name was raised on every lip. Whoever saw the procession pass by, men, women and children, shed new tears for the departed great man as the cortege advanced, followed by tear-filled eyes. Boys stood at attention while the famous Rav passed by; the

Rav Salant in his old age

*The facade of Yeshivath Porath Yosef facing the
Western Wall*

younger ones, who had never seen the Rav outside, drank in his holiness with their eyes as an event to remember for the rest of their lives. All the students of the Sefaradi yeshiva, Porath Yosef, lined the balconies of the immense building and threw kisses in Rav Shmuel's direction. And even the Arabs stood at attention and bowed as the Rav's chair crossed their path, for when Rav Shmuel had been younger they had been wont to bring their litigation to the Jewish judge for mediation.

By the time Rav Shmuel reached his destination, a huge crowd had accumulated behind him. He entered and sat beside Rav Ben-Zion, the only son of the deceased.

"Oy! What is the month of Elul — the month of repentance — without Reb Hirsh Michel!" he moaned, "the Ten Days of Teshuva without Reb Hirsh Michel... Rosh haShanah and the Day of Holiness without him... Sukkoth, Hoshana Rabba and Simchath Torah without the *tzaddik*!"

The tiny room was packed with those who had accompanied Rav Shmuel. The air was suffocating. A low keening set off the Rav's words, low enough to be heard but not loud enough to interfere with Rav Shmuel's dirge.

"Who can give us his *tefilla*, his *tikkun chatzoth*, his particular observance to the letter of each mitzva, his tireless devotion to study, his asceticism... What is Jerusalem, the holy city, without the presence of Rav Hirsh Michel?"

Silence reigned and then again an undercurrent of wailing.

Rav Shmuel arose and turned to the practical aspect of his visit. "Have the following inscription engraved upon your father's tombstone," he instructed Rav Ben-Zion: " 'The glory of the Holy Land, he never accepted any appointment.' "

156

Rav Shmuel pronounced the traditional condolence wish and began to leave. In an instant his bodyguards lifted him high on his chair, placed the chair on their shoulders and proceeded to return to his house in the courtyard adjoining the Churva *shul.* And that was the last time he ever crossed his own threshold alive.

When Rav Shmuel reached home, his faithful doctor was already waiting for him. Upon learning of the Rav's excursion, this *tzaddik* of a doctor, Reb Moshe Wallach, had hurried to be present for his return.

"Reb Moshe, what do you say to the blow that has fallen so suddenly upon our holy city?" Rav Shmuel asked his visitor. "Do you have any conception of how much *yirath shamayim* and heavenly service will be lacking now in Jerusalem with the demise of Rav Hirsh Michel?" The doctor did not answer the question. He tried instead to calm the excited Rav, for his present state of emotional upheaval was detrimental to his health. Reb Moshe Wallach tried to change the subject but Rav Shmuel would not be calmed. Instead he burst into a fresh stream of tears.

The trusty physician stayed by the Rav's bedside until he had somewhat calmed down. He then arose to leave but Rav Shmuel detained him.

"Come, stay here a bit. Let me tell you something that will convince you of the loss that Jerusalem has incurred.

"The saintly Rav Nachum of Sadik used to study *Gemara* regularly with one of the *tzaddikim* of Jerusalem. In the course of their studies they once came across the homiletic explanation of the Sages on the verse, 'In hiding does my soul weep.' There exists a specific place designated as God's 'hiding-place,' the Sages say. There He weeps over the Kingdom of Heaven that has been exiled. Rav Nachum trembled when he read this. He reviewed this midrash over and over again, weeping absorbedly. He could not overcome his emotions until he had decided to secure a small hiding-place in this world where those who grieved for the exile of the Divine Presence could come and let their grief spill over into prayer before God.

"The Spring of Shiloach by the Mount of Olives is traditionally reputed to have been the immersion *mikveh* of Rabbi Yishmael the Kohein Gadol. Nearby is a ruin situated so as to be hidden from the public eye. Lying in a courtyard within a courtyard, this ruin was designated as that very hiding-place. Its entrance was fitted with a special lock fashioned by a locksmith who cast special copper keys to fit it. These keys were entrusted to an elite group of men who had purified their eyes and minds from tainted sights and thoughts from the day they had reached maturity. And in the Jerusalem that was then all purity and holiness, only thirteen *tzaddikim* were found worthy of possessing such keys.

"And," Rav Shmuel concluded feelingly, "one of the thirteen possessors of a key was Rav Hirsh Michel. He was one of the pillars of the city of holiness."

Reb Moshe Wallach was deeply moved by this story. Only now did he begin to understand the loss that Jerusalem had incurred with the demise of Rav Hirsh Michel. Reb Moshe, who had been an ardent follower of Rav Chayim Sonnenfeld ever since his immigration to the holy land, felt compelled to ask,

"Is it permitted for the Rav to reveal if my teacher and master, Rav Yosef Chayim Sonnenfeld, is among those thirteen?"

"What a question! What a question!" Rav Shmuel

repeated. "Hasn't Rav Chayim been the first and fore-most in everything holy?"

Thoroughly overcome with emotion, Dr. Wallach took his leave of Rav Shmuel and hurried to the house of his *rebbi*, Rav Chayim Sonnenfeld. After begging for a quick *bracha* that he succeed in his healing, he continued on to his daily routine at the hospital.

The story of the copper keys became public knowledge. The only non-possessor, however, who knew who still possessed one of those cherished keys was Reb Moshe Wallach. And he told no one.

Dr. Moshe Wallach with the Rav of Jerusalem,
Rav Yosef Tzvi Dushinski

Dr. Moshe Wallach in his surgery

A Boy's Future Predicted

IF RAV YOSEF Chayim Sonnenfeld had been given a priceless copper key to the Place of Hiding, it was not without reason. For one thing, he stemmed from holy seed. His father, his grandfather, and the generations preceding them had all held coveted rabbinical positions in communities of repute. But despite all this, Rav Chayim built his reputation, his spiritual world, all by himself.

He had suffered a difficult childhood. Before he was four, his father passed away, and his mother, saddled with other hungry children, saw no way out but to remarry. Chayim's stepfather was completely different from the man his father had been. A rabbi, the son of rabbis, Chayim's father would have wished to see his son continue the family tradition and grow up to be a leader of Jewry. His stepfather had different plans for the precocious little boy; he wanted the child to develop his talents in famous universities and gain world recognition via doctorates and academic titles.

The crisis was not long in coming, and when it came it proved to be the turning point in Chayim's life. The occasion was the visit of Rav Yehuda Assad to Chayim's town. A world-renowned *tzaddik*, the author of *Teshuvoth Yehuda Ya'aleh*, he was accorded royal honor. The city went all out in erecting triumphal arches along the main streets. Huge signs reading WELCOME and A TZADDIK COMES

TO THE CITY were displayed in central locations. Semnitz seethed with preparations and expectations.

On the momentous day hundreds lined the street the *tzaddik* would pass through. The scholars of Semnitz came with their talmudic problems and queries; the merchants came to glean near-prophetic advice; the wealthy came with *pidyonoth* to give the visiting celebrity, while the poor came to beg for donations. But the majority of the assembled masses were the simple people, the common folk. Old men dragged themselves to beseech a *bracha* for longevity; women with babes in arms hoped to get close enough for the Rav to place his blessed hands upon the tiny heads of their children.

Chayim could not help wishing he were a part of all this activity. The more he heard about the *tzaddik*, the more he wished to receive his own personal blessing. But who would take the young boy? Not his mother, who was busy with house and children. Not his stepfather, surely. And his father — he was gone five years already. Alone? He would be trodden under the masses of people twice his size, twice his bulk. Never mind. Chayim was too bright to let the problem get him down. He was determined to go. And if no one would or could take him, he would have to go alone.

Inch by inch the boy wormed his way through the crowd until he finally reached the front lines where he could see the celebrity with his own eyes. When he actually stood before Rav Yehuda, the great man could not help noticing the unusual child staring up at him.

"Where is your father, my child?" he asked Chayim.

Chayimka blushed and answered with lowered head. "I am an orphan, the son of Rav Shlomo the son of Rav Shmuel of Jergen. I have come to you for a blessing. I want to attain greatness in Torah and in fear of God."

The great man was profoundly moved by the words that emerged from a pure heart, and no less by the identity of the speaker. But the pushing, insistent crowd did not permit him more than a quick blessing. Placing his hands upon the head of the little boy with the penentrating eyes and noble features, he said, "May you succeed in continuing the golden chain that your family has forged. May you grow to be a Torah giant and a leader of your generation."

The Rav had a long line of people waiting for his blessing and so he turned away from the child. But Chayim did not have other things to occupy his mind. The famous man had made a deep, indelible impression on his soul, the *tzaddik* even more than his blessing. A new spirit entered Chayim's soul. He was suddenly filled with a new joy for life, and from that joy began to sprout a purpose, a plan. Chayim determined to run away.

Chayim's mother learned of his plan and did not offer resistance. In fact, she even encouraged the boy. Although her mother's heart ached at the thought of parting with her dear child, she was glad that he would be going to a Torah center where he could grow in wisdom. She packed a few belongings and the boy was off for Verbau, his birthplace.

Chayim went all alone, to study in the yeshiva of Rav Chayim Tzvi Mannheimer, the Torah personality who later became Rav of Ungvar (Uzhorod). The *rosh ha-yeshiva* welcomed the boy with open arms, for he had known his father and his grandfather, and he pinned great hopes on the youth. "Torah returns to its customary hostel," he said. Not many days passed before he was convinced of it. The boy soon acquired a name as the choice scholar of all Hungarian yeshivoth.

From Rav Chayim Tzvi's yeshiva he went on to study

under the Kethav Sofer in Pressburg. He immediately earned a good name but he never forgot his unhappy childhood. When he discovered a poor, lonely widow, he did her Friday shopping for her every week, and wished her a hearty *Gut Shaboss*, while she showered endless blessings upon his young head.

His spiritual success was evident at once. Not so pleasant were his material circumstances. The temporary quarters that were assigned to him outside the yeshiva were uncomfortable, to say the least. His host was a well-intending but impoverished man who could offer no better accommodations than shaky boards laid across some poles for a bed. It was narrow and very incommodious.

Several days after his arrival in Pressburg the director of the yeshiva met Chayim. "How are you, Chayim?" he asked the youth who had captured the hearts of all his beholders. He thumped him on the back in friendly manner, "And how are your temporary quarters?"

"Wonderful," came the quick reply. "But I am distressed over one thing — that I cannot properly observe the first paragraph of the *Shulchan Aruch* that bids a man when he arises in the morning to 'be brave like a lion to perform his heavenly duties.' I need to gather no courage to jump out of my bed. It is easier to get out of it than to lie in it."

But physical circumstances did not prevent Chayim from growing spiritually and attaining Torah scholarship. His *rebbi*, the Kethav Sofer, soon became strongly attached to the boy and made him a steady guest at his Shabbath table. The Kethav Sofer once laid his hand on Chayim's head and said, "Your name is Chayim and the numerical value of Chayim is equivalent to that of *chacham*." At first the youth shied away from such a show of attention and affection. He was simply afraid of the honor that came his way. But he soon grew accustomed to the demonstrations of love and became like a dear son to his *rebbi*.

The *rosh ha-yeshiva*'s love for his star pupil expressed itself in another way. Whenever a visitor wanted to see the products of the yeshiva, it was Chayim who was summoned first to give a favorable impression.

The spa city of Auben, some distance from Pressburg, was the site of a concentration of much Torah greatness during the summer months. Numerous tales were told about the heavenly matters discussed among the Torah celebrities who visited there. Although many merchants also made this spa their vacation spot, the center of attention was always the Torah personalities. In addition, they attracted lesser Torah personalities who found the time and place opportune for posing their most difficult talmudic problems or halachic questions. The greater the celebrity who made his appearance, the greater was the crowd of people that he attracted.

Word got around that the famous author of *Teshuvoth Divrey Chayim*, the Rav and Rebbe of Tzanz, was expected. Rabbanim and *roshay yeshiva* and their disciples began streaming *en masse* to greet the sage and talk to him face to face. They came armed with their toughest questions and most problematic riddles, partly to impress and partly to let themselves be impressed. The Kethav Sofer was not one to be left out. He felt it his duty to send a representative group from his yeshiva to impress the *Divrey Chayim* and thereby enhance the memory of the yeshiva's founder, his father, the Chatham Sofer.

The chosen group, Chayim Sonnenfeld among them, set out for Auben. The Rav of Tzanz received them with the respect due their yeshiva. But his eyes kept singling out the star of the group, Chayim Sonnenfeld, who felt the holy eyes on him, too.

An invisible bond was formed between the two upon that occasion. Later, when Chayim was summoned to appear before the draft board, he headed first to Tzanz to ask the Rebbe for his blessing and to beg the *tzaddik* to mention him in his prayers. As soon as he reached the Rebbe's house he was personally greeted at the threshold.

"So they want to make a general out of you?" the Rebbe asked. "But you are designated to become a general of Jewry in Eretz Yisrael!"

A ringing silence followed these words. All the people at the Rebbe's court waited to hear what else the *Divrey Chayim* would say in his commanding voice. "When you return home, be sure to bandage your feet," he said enigmatically and bade the youth farewell.

Doubly surprised, infinitely impressed, the youth left the *tzaddik's* house. In his modesty, he felt the prophetic blessing to be of no great personal significance. But he could not begin to understand what the Rav had meant about the bandages. With full measure of confidence in *tzaddikim*, Chayim was certain that this advice had significance and that there was no need to return and inquire further.

As he reached the crossroads, Chayim felt thousands of pins and needles penetrating his body, especially his feet. Chayim was a man capable of suffering in silence but this overpowering itching was more than he could bear. From minute to minute it grew worse; his feet swelled increasingly. By the time he got to the draft board his limping, aching feet could barely hold him up. He was in the examination room and out in the span of half an hour, emerging with an exemption certificate and the solicitous advice of the doctor that he hurry home to care for his feet before their condition proved critical enough to endanger his very life.

Chayim, of course, was not concerned about his condition. He turned to go home in a peaceful state of mind, waiting for the first opportunity to fulfill the Rav's counsel. The minute he set painful foot into his house he began to wind bandages around his feet, around and around. As he wound the roll of gauze about his foot he could feel the pain subsiding, the swelling easing, the itching vanishing. By the time he had completed the dressing, his feet were back to normal.

The Kethav Sofer

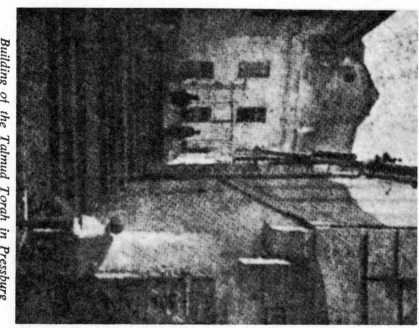

Building of the Talmud Torah in Pressburg

In Abraham's Tent

THE NAME OF THE choicest, most eligible young man in
the Pressburg yeshiva travelled far and wide. Rich men,
men of lineage, rabbis, and community leaders competed
to marry off their daughters to Chayim Sonnenfeld. The
Kethav Sofer even put in a good word for one of these
proposed matches, but Chayim decided that such a
momentous step must be his own choice. When he was
finally offered the daughter of a modest Jew who served
as a *shochet* in one of the Hungarian communities, he
agreed immediately. He explained that the "daughters of
rich men are accustomed to comforts which — were
to marry one — I would have to provide. This is not
the case with the daughter of a modest man who will be
satisfied with a lower standard of this-worldly living."

And it happened more than once after his marriage,
when the last penny had been spent, that Rav Chayim
sat down with his young wife at the supper table — to
"dine" on a lesson in *Mesilath Yesharim* or *Chovoth ha-
Levavoth*.

One worry alone nagged at the young *chathan*. Although
truly grateful that he had found a mate to suit him, he
was ashamed that he owned no suit to appear in at the
yeshiva when he would be called to the Torah on the
Shabbath before his wedding. It wasn't the lack of the suit
that bothered Chayim. He was far beyond such petty
considerations as personal pride in appearance. He was

afraid, however, that when his *rebbi*, the Kethav Sofer, would notice that even on this Shabbath he wore shreds and patches, he would force charity money on him to buy a decent suit. And taking from charity, accepting gifts, was something completely contrary and abhorrent to his nature. But the clever Chayim found a way out as usual. He appeared so late to prayers on the Shabbath preceding his wedding, that he had to be called up as he was — in one of the communal synagogues of the city.

Chayim parted with his beloved *rebbi* in Adar, 5630. The leavetaking of two closely-knit souls, that of *rebbi* and beloved disciple, is a difficult one. At that occasion the Kethav Sofer handed his pupil a completely handwritten *semicha*, the labor of his own hand.

Rav Yosef Chayim later related an interesting sidelight about this *semicha* — one of the most laudatory *semichoth* ever given by the Kethav Sofer. Afraid that its contents might go to his head, Chayim kept the document in its original folds for some twenty years. Only when he was forty years of age did he dare read it or show it to someone else, for by then he felt that even such a certification would not influence him to undue pride.

After his marriage, Rav Chayim went to live near his father-in-law. The Rav of the city was Rav Avraham Shag, author of *Ohel Avraham*. He incorporated the young man into his circle of disciples. Rav Chayim later said that those years of study under Rav Avraham "were of tremendous value. During that period I was inculcated with valuable character traits and a lifestyle that have remained with me ever since." Rav Avraham himself was a perfect man. He encompassed the full spectrum of all desirable traits and virtues, setting a shining example for the young man whom he loved as a son. Small wonder, then, that when Rav Avraham declared his intention to ascend to the Holy Land, Rav Chayim did not hesitate to follow.

Rav Chayim used to tell his confidants about that decision. He never would have contemplated going to Eretz Yisrael on his own. He felt, at the time, that he was far from ready and worthy to live in the Holy Land and absorb its rarefied atmosphere of purity. But neither could he part from his beloved *rebbi*. His decision to accompany Rav Avraham also stemmed from a desire to be of service to him and ease the travails of the difficult journey.

In preparation for the trip, Rav Chayim studied and perfected himself in *shechita* so that his *rebbi* would never have to be without meat for Shabbath.

Rav Avraham had originally planned to take an elite contingency of the Chatham Sofer's disciples to form a Torah core in the Holy Land, in the manner of the Baal Shem Tov's and the Vilna Gaon's *talmidim*. When this plan did not work out, he was not overly disappointed for, as he told his close acquaintances, "The one disciple I will take along will do more to enhance the sacredness of Jerusalem than all of them together could have done."

A tremendous measure of self-sacrifice was required for this peril-filled journey. For six long weeks the ship teetered from side to side in rough seas, but Rav Chayim had been prepared for this, too, and did not leave his *rebbi's* side, nor regret the decision that had brought him there.

Little did the young disciple realize that with this trip he was embarking upon a future of accompanying the Holy Land's Torah-true Jews on their upward journey to the House of God. Nor did he realize that the ship which harbored him and his *rebbi* was a vessel that would ensure the persistence of orthodox Jewry in Jerusalem and Eretz Yisrael.

During the entire trip, the two travelers immersed themselves in the laws pertaining to Eretz Yisrael and in describing its virtues, for Rav Avraham intended spending the rest of his days in this gateway to heaven. The last few days were the hardest, for then their anticipation was heightened. As soon as the captain announced that the ship was approaching the shore, Rav Chayim bounded up to the upper deck and climbed up to the crow's-nest in order to catch the very first glimpse of the long-awaited shore. Then he scrambled down to invite his *rebbi* up on the deck, and to announce that he had fulfilled the verse, "You will see the land from afar."

Rav Avraham Shag

Rav Yehoshua Leib Diskin

In the Rav of Brisk's Shadow

THE SACRED CITY embraced Rav Shag and his disciple with loving arms. Rav Avraham, alas, did not live long after his immigration. He was summoned to join the heavenly yeshiva, and Rav Chayim was orphaned once again from a loving father. This time, however, he was not impeded. There were other giants to whom to turn, and he chose Rav Meir Auerbach and Rav Shmuel Salant; and later, when that eminent personality graced Jerusalem with his holy presence, Rav Yehoshua Leib Diskin, the Rav of Brisk. And he, in turn, became the Brisker Rav's star disciple.

The Rav of Brisk waged an aggressive, uncompromising battle against the destroyers of traditional Jewish education, and against parents who enrolled their children in secular schools established by the freethinkers from abroad. Rav Chayim was appointed the general of this battle. He was sent to convince parents of the gravity of the situation; he was sent to enforce the ban against the schools and their founders; he was the man when it came to action of any sort on this battleground.

It was a fierce fight with no compromising. When the *gabbai* of the Churva synagogue lay on his deathbed, Rav Yehoshua Leib Diskin was approached to pray for him. He refused, point blank. His reason — the *gabbai* had objected to Rav Chayim announcing the ban on secular schools in the Churva synagogue.

174

Upon another occasion a huge sum of money was sent by a wealthy Hungarian Jew to be apportioned among ten Torah scholars of the Hungarian Kolel. Lots were thrown for the prize but one of the ten winners was disqualified when it was learned that his grandchild attended a secular school. Rav Chayim, the president of the Kolel, refused to enrich a man whose grandson violated the Rav of Brisk's ban of having nothing to do with the schools. Other members of the board of directors argued for the tenth man. It was not the grandfather's fault, they said. The man's relatives finally took the case to the Rav of Brisk himself. When he heard the case he asked shortly, "Is the grandson supported by his grandfather?" When an affirmative reply was given he nodded, "Then Rav Chayim is right."

A similar story was told by the Rav of Brisk's disciples, but with a different conclusion. Rav Chayim was once invited to a *brith* made by one of Rav Yehoshua Leib's disciples. Complications arose when it was discovered that the mother of the child was closely related to a freethinker who had waged an unholy war for the opposite camp. It was certain that he would attend the joyous event and would have to be honored with participation in the ceremony. In order to avoid a confrontation, the young father planned to perform the *brith* one hour before scheduled. He informed Rav Chayim of the change of plans, and bade him come an hour before. To his surprise, Rav Chayim vigorously opposed the change since it would cause unnecessary aggravation to the mother, and might endanger her and the child. "Despite my staunch opposition to this particular relative, we may not endanger innocent lives."

When the father still held to his position, Rav Chayim suggested that he go to the Rav of Brisk and ask his

advice. To the father's compound amazement, the Rav up-
held his disciple's decision. This firebrand of a zealot
agreed that it was not worth the risk to the mother and
that the *brith* should proceed as originally scheduled.

Rav of Jerusalem

WHEN RAV YEHOSHUA LEIB DISKIN passed away, Rav Chayim was pressured to accept the rabbinical position. Rav Shmuel Salant, then greatly weakened by old age, sought a helper and urged those close to him to "hurry and crown Rav Chayim." But Rav Chayim shied away from prestigious positions for most of his life. Only in his later years, when the opponents of Judaism threatened to gain supremacy over the institution of the rabbinate, was Rav Chayim compelled to accept the honored post of Rav of Jerusalem.

Jerusalem was not in specific need of Rav Chayim's genius or his halachic decisions. It blossomed as fully with Torah giants and halachic colossi as it had when the Rav of Brisk had made his appearance on the scene. All throughout his life in the Diaspora, Rav Yehoshua Leib had headed a yeshiva and propagated Torah. But when he arrived in Jerusalem, he set all aside. Once in Jerusalem he specifically dedicated all his talents to preserving the purity of Jewish education. He founded an orphan home to teach Torah and a trade to every orphan. He descended from the heights to come closer to Jewish youth. Left behind were the careers of Torah and yeshiva, for in Jerusalem he had more important work to do. His new task was to guard the city walls from those who threatened to storm the fortress.

The 'stormers of the fortress' of those days were not at all like the modern-day enemies of religion. A short-bearded Jew or one without *tzitzith*, much less a bare-headed Jew, would have made no headway whatsoever against Jerusalem Jewry. Anyone with designs against religion had to go in roundabout fashion. He was forced to sport a long beard, and he had to be familiar with the sayings of our Sages. A battle against such impostors was sevenfold harder. But Rav Chayim, like his master, did not fear them, and he soon made short shrift of their posturing.

A serious confrontation occurred in the year 5642 with the visit of the French founder of the Alliance Israélite Universelle movement. The purpose of the visit was to strengthen the hands of Nissim Bachar, the Sefaradi activist, and founder of the Alliance secular school in Jerusalem. The visitor made his first appearance on Shabbath in the Churva synagogue where some people, sympathetic to his cause, arranged a coveted place for him on the eastern wall.

A blackguard of this caliber required a man of penetrating foresight for an opponent. Such a man was not lacking. That very Shabbath, the Rav of Brisk summoned Rav Chayim to him and bade him hasten to the Churva synagogue, accompanied by two other disciples, Rav Yaakov Orenstein and Rav Yitzchak Shlomo Blau. There he was to proclaim the ban on secular schools in the presence of the entire congregation before the reading of the Torah.

The three went forth. When they arrived they found their way barred by a gang of hoodlums who surrounded the synagogue on all sides. Rav Chayim was the only one who succeeded in penetrating the infamous ring. He pushed his way through the packed crowd, strode purposefully up to the platform and proclaimed the ban in ringing tones. He had barely finished his message when

Rav Yosef Chayim Sonnenfeld

he was brutally attacked by the ruffians. By a miracle alone, he escaped with his life through the confusion that reigned in the crowded synagogue but he bore the telltale signs on his body long afterwards, and would refer to them as "medals I won for valiance on the field of battle."

This event had its echoes even after Rav Chayim's death. Two weeks after a secular school building collapsed in Jaffa, some passersby found a severed hand among the ruins. It was brought to Rav Yosef Tzvi HaLeivi, the Rav of Jaffa, to decide what should be done with it, since it was thought to be the hand of one of the veteran teachers who had probably been buried alive under the wreckage.

Rav Yosef Tzvi examined the hand, the wristwatch and the fragment of the shirt sleeve that remained on it. As he heard the testimony identifying the man, he fainted. When he was revived, he exclaimed in a fearful tone: "Who can begin to imagine the extent of God's justice! This is the very hand that many years ago struck Rav Yosef Chayim Sonnenfeld when he proclaimed the ban on schools on that memorable Shabbath in the Churva shul."

Symbol of Purity

RAV CHAYIM WAS A MAN in whom good traits clustered.
Consummate in every human virtue, a giant in Torah
knowledge, a *tzaddik* in the full sense of the word, Rav
Chayim also incorporated a fierce fighting spirit for the
sacred traditions of the Jewish people. But his uncompromising nature did not overshadow his gentler virtues. He
was a man of unsurpassed goodheartedness and loving-
kindness for his fellowman. Not only were the direct
beneficiaries of his goodness aware of his exemplary modesty and warmth; even those who had exchanged the
briefest words with the *tzaddik* were immediately cog-
nizant of the noble generosity of spirit that was a vital part
of the man. From the light shining forth from his noble
face upon every person, from his diligent efforts to encourage
and inspire every creature of Godly form, it was apparent
to all around him that he was a bubbling fount of goodness
and blessing.

Rav Chayim made himself beloved of all Jerusalem's inhabitants, young and old alike, common and
important, municipal figures and simple folk. Everyone
found in the *tzaddik* a soulmate or a kind father, as his
need required. The lonely, the childless, the bitter, the dis-
illusioned all found at his address a heart and hearth
where they could warm their souls.

His marvelous virtues were all evident before he was
proclaimed the Rav of Jerusalem, before he became

known as the supreme authority of the Holy Land. As his fame grew, his virtues expanded. And these were revealed in an extraordinary occurrence a short time after he was crowned Rav of Jerusalem.

Rav Chayim lived in a basement apartment which one had to descend several steps to reach. His house was in the Batey Machseh section of the Old City and his windows were on the same level as the Har haBayith. Above his home were the offices of the Kolel Amsterdam, an address which was well known to the citizens of Batey Machseh, just as Reb Yisrael Lobel, the Kolel's secretary and manager, was a familiar personality on the Jerusalem scene.

One Friday afternoon Reb Yisrael suddenly reminded himself that Mrs. Rosenfeld, who lived on the third floor of that building, was eligible for a subsidy that had arrived on her name. He asked his assistant to go upstairs and ask the woman to come down to the office and receive the money due her.

This assistant was neither great sage nor little fool. First of all, he confused the name Rosenfeld with Sonnenfeld. Then he confused the upstairs with downstairs. In short, he went to Rav Chayim instead of to Mrs. Rosenfeld and delivered his message, "Reb Yisrael Lobel asks that you come up to his office."

On the spot, the Rav of Jerusalem took his seventy years, his genius, and his dignity and went up the stairs to Reb Yisrael. When the door opened and the Rav stepped in, Reb Yisrael nearly fainted.

"W-what," he began, stammering. "What is the Rav of Jerusalem doing in my office? If he required my presence," he continued in the respectful third person, "he should have sent for me. I would have come immediately. Why did the Rav inconvenience himself?"

Rav Yosef Chayim Sonnefeld visiting the newly built Hadassah Hospital in Jerusalem, accompanied by Rav Moshe Blau and the hospital's director, Dr. Yaski. Rav Yosef Chayim saw the founding of every new Jewish hospital as a bulwark against medical care by missionary hospitals

Rav Chayim answered simply, "Your assistant came to summon me, and here I am. What can I do for you?"

Reb Yisrael grew even more flustered. "Would anyone begin to imagine that I should send for the Rav of Jerusalem to appear before me? Am I crazy? Or do I lack the proper respect for the Torah, God forbid? Am I so low in the Rav's opinion that he suspects me of either?"

In midspeech Reb Yisrael suddenly figured out the puzzle. "Oy!" he exclaimed in utter horror and "Oy!" again. "My stupid assistant must have confused the names Sonnenfeld and Rosenfeld and gone to summon the Rav." He begged the Rav's forgiveness a thousand times for having violated the respect due the Torah, albeit in error. He then explained the circumstances to Rav Chayim, promising to give his stupid assistant something by which to remember his idiocy.

The Rav again took his seventy years, his august position, and his holiness and pleaded with every nuance, word, and argument he knew that the assistant's feelings not be hurt. "Such a mistake can happen to any man," he explained and, saying goodbye, left.

But he didn't go downstairs. Instead he went one flight up, to Mrs. Rosenfeld. He knocked on her door and informed the woman that Reb Yisrael of the Kolel Amsterdam below had some money for her, and wished her to come and get it.

This golden tale did not appear suddenly on the horizon. And it was only one of many brilliant gems that glittered in Rav Chayim's crown of glory. Rav Chayim stories still circulate in Jerusalem society. Jerusalem's old-timers love to tell of the citizen who once arose to view the sunrise from his window but filled his eyes instead with the strange sight of Jerusalem's Rav hurrying by with two pails dangling from a pole on his shoulders, like a professional water-carrier. He was delivering water to a desolate widow who lived all alone in an adjoining courtyard.

Yerushalmim enjoy even more telling of the time a man opened his door one morning in answer to a knock outside. Who should he see but Rav Chayim, burdened with two pails brimful of water, requesting entry to deposit his dripping load.

What had happened? As the flabbergasted citizen learned by rushing out immediately and hurrying after Rav Chayim, his wife had gone to the nearby well to fill her pails, dragging her children behind her. She filled the pails, and then took one child along with her, leaving the others with the pails to await her return. The children attempted to drag the pails by themselves until Rav Chayim came along, hoisted the pails on his own shoulders and marched home.

When the man caught up with Rav Chayim, who had hurried along on his way, he could find no words with which to express his shame and his regret at being served by the great man. But his eyes spoke for him; the tears rolled swiftly down his cheeks. When Rav Chayim saw his distress, he calmed him,

"It really surprises me that adults begrudge me the mitzva of *azov ta'azov*, which comes my way rarely enough. Yet Jewish children gladly grant me opportunity to fulfill this mitzva."

Another favorite story concerns the head of the rabbinical court, Rav Moshe Nachum Wallenstein, who occasionally had to go abroad for communal purposes and leave behind his wife with a houseful of young children. Rav Chayim would enter the courtyard of their home early each morning and deposit a can of warm coffee with

185

milk, after which he would slip out quietly without anyone knowing the identity of the kindly milkman.

Rav Chayim's household once went looking for Rav Chayim and found him in his Yom Tov clothing, performing the wedding of two unfortunate, feeble-minded people whom the other rabbanim of the city had refused to join together. But this was not enough for Rav Chayim; he felt he also had to dance for the "honorable *chathan* and *kalla*" and gladden their hearts until late into the night.

"First and foremost," Rav Shmuel Salant had once said of Rav Chayim, "for anything of sanctity." This was one of the giants of Jerusalem chosen to possess the coveted copper key to the Place of Hiding.

With General Masaryk — the president of Czechoslovakia

ירושלים של מעלה

In the Footsteps
of the Original
Settlers

Rich Man, Poor Man, and the
Rav of Jerusalem

THE NAME ASHER TRACHTENBERG was well known in the old circles of Jerusalem. A wealthy man hailing from Elizabeth, New Jersey, Trachtenberg generously supported the many religious educational institutions in the Old City. Although he himself did not study Torah, he harbored a strong sentiment and deep love for the Torah studied there. This attachment was acquired from his stepfather who, having raised him from childhood on, had inculcated in him a deep respect for Torah and mitzvoth.

After many years of supporting the institutions in the Old City, Asher Trachtenberg developed a desire to visit the Holy Land. For the wealthy philanthropist it was a simple step from inclination to realization, and one Elul found him inside the city gates, leisurely promenading along the narrow streets and in the covered marketplaces.

The secretary of the Etz Chayim yeshiva, representing the beneficiary of huge sums, was informed beforehand of Mr. Trachtenberg's visit and hurried to the visitor's hotel. The secretary suggested to his wealthy guest that he pay a visit to Rav Shmuel Salant, then Rav of Jerusalem and head of the yeshiva. When Mr. Trachtenberg willingly agreed, they went together to Rav Shmuel's home.

One did not require a previous appointment with the

Rav. His home was open to all, any time of the day or night. The secretary announced Mr. Trachtenberg and introduced him to the Rav as one of the main supporters of the yeshiva. The Rav welcomed him warmly, as was his way, and listened politely while the visitor outlined his past efforts on behalf of many Jerusalem institutions and elaborated on his future plans. Rav Shmuel enthusiastically encouraged the philanthropist.

In the midst of their conversation, a tap was heard on the outer door and Rav Shmuel asked the secretary to invite the visitor in. The guest sat down in the outer room and awaited his turn.

"Who is it?" the rabbi asked casually.

"The young Polish fellow," answered the secretary.

The Rav, evidently excited over the identity of his visitor, was out of his seat and in the adjoining room in a flash. He ushered the young man in and begged him to sit down, embracing him and leaning over him solicitously. Only when the newcomer was comfortably settled at his right side, did Rav Shmuel finally relax.

It is not easy to describe the young yeshiva scholar. He was desperately poor, as evidenced by his ragged clothing; his shoes, though heavily mended, were falling apart; his shapeless hat fell below his forehead; his trousers were held up by a belt of red handkerchiefs joined together end to end. As for his facial features — his eyes were sunk deeply into their sockets, and his split lower lip revealed a set of raven-black teeth. Despite these shortcomings, his face shone.

"What do you want, my dear Reb Hirshele?" Rav Shmuel asked him with a surprising degree of affection.

"Nothing special, really, rebbi," answered the young scholar. "I simply wanted to suggest a fitting answer for the question that Rabbi Akiva Eiger poses in his Gilyon on Mishnayoth. It struck me just this morning while I was waiting my turn at the eye clinic."

"Well, well," Rav Shmuel joked, "a Torah commentary developed at the eye clinic should be quite enlightened! By all means, let's hear the explanation that struck you at the eye clinic!"

The young scholar opened his mouth and let the words flow. And as commonly happens, one thought followed upon the heels of another, a comment aroused a counter-comment from Rav Shmuel and, before they realized it. they were both deep in halachic discussion. Their conversation went on for about half an hour, the two men so engrossed that they were oblivious of the third party who had been sitting there silently all the long while. Mr. Trachtenberg was not a person used to being ignored. He smarted at the slight to his dignity, all the greater in view of the appearance of the man who had replaced him in the Rav's attention. The smarting turned to anger and the philanthropist lashed out caustically, "I doubt if in America a similar incident would take place. I doubt if a rabbi, a celebrated personality, would make a to-do over a young beggar."

As the words left Mr. Trachtenberg's mouth and entered Rav Shmuel's ears, the latter underwent a transformation. His body shook and he arose in a rage. Shouting and striking his fist on the table, he turned to the American, "How dare you express yourself thus about a young *talmid chacham,* a scholar of the yeshiva? This is sheer arrogance, arrogance beyond measure!"

The members of Rav Shmuel's household shook with fear, for it was rare that he was provoked into anger. The secretary of the yeshiva tried at once to mollify the Rav, but he refused to calm down.

He did contain his anger for a few minutes, during

which he remained silent. Then he turned to the secretary and directed his next words to him, "Why do we honor wealthy people altogether? Is it not so that they can help us cultivate young men such as this one? For they are the ones, in the end, who uphold the very world! But if the wealthy denigrate and abuse the Torah scholars, then who needs them? Who needs them? I strongly feel that he should be properly censured. Does he think it a small thing to express such thoughts?! To embarrass a Torah scholar?! And before the Rav, yet!"

The philanthropist did not wait to hear more. He rose abruptly and walked out, leaving the secretary to bemoan the loss of such a valuable supporter. To all appearances, the profitable relationship had been permanently severed.

Reb Hirshele

AND WHO WAS REB HIRSHELE, the young man whose honor Rav Shmuel defended so fiercely?

Born in Warsaw, Poland, Reb Hirshele had studied under Rav Yitzchak Me'ir, the Rebbe of Gur, and the author of *Chiddushey haRim*. A great scholar in his own right, Reb Hirshele was afflicted with poverty and physical ailments alike. When his brother died in Jerusalem without leaving offspring to carry on his name, Reb Hirshele immigrated together with his family, primarily to give his brother's widow a proper *chalitza,* but also to spend the rest of his life in the Holy City. To this purpose his *rebbi,* the *Chiddushey haRim,* supplied the young man with a letter of recommendation to Rav Shmuel Salant.

The letter was brief:

"I hereby testify that this young man, bearer of this letter, has been studying Torah through hardship ever since he has attained maturity. He blackens his face in the toil of Torah for its own sake. Kindly befriend him and help him."

The *Chiddushey haRim* handed Reb Hirshele the letter unsealed so that he could give it directly to Reb Shmuel. After taking and folding it into his pocket, he said his final goodbyes.

When Reb Hirshele was on board ship and in the middle of the ocean, he was suddenly seized with an urge to read the contents of the letter, seeing that it was open. He

wanted to see his *rebbi*'s holy handwriting and read the
Torah thoughts that he was certain the letter contained.
Why else would the letter have been open, he reasoned,
if not that it contained no personal message. He opened
his belt and took the letter out from an inner pocket.

As soon as he began to read the letter's contents, he
felt ashamed that such words had been written about
him. Now a violent inner conflict was launched for Reb
Hirshele. Should he after all, deliver the letter to Rav
Shmuel? Or should he destroy it? If he transmitted it,
he would, in effect, be using his Torah as a cutting axe,
as a tool with which to gain fame and a livelihood. His
mind swarmed with stringent warnings from the Sages
against utilizing one's Torah knowledge for material or
personal purposes. He recalled an incident concerning
Rabbi Tarfon in which he was seized and almost killed
by a kidnaper. Rabbi Tarfon pleaded with the kidnaper
to save his life but to no avail. He then revealed his
identity, thus saving his neck. Rabbi Tarfon regretted this
action, however, for the rest of his life, for he had used
the crown of Torah for a personal end. Reb Hirshele remembered the saying in *Pirkey Avoth*, "He who uses the
crown of Torah will die." These and many more such
thoughts raced through his head. But doubt ate into him.
By delivering the letter he was fulfilling his *rebbi's* charge.
Reb Hirshele did not concern himself wth the aspect of
a livelihood; that did not play a role in his considerations.
Yet somehow he felt that with the delivery of the letter
he would be wiping away all of his Torah merit and piety,
as if he were erasing a full slate.

The ship was sailing at a fast clip along the ocean waves.
A cool wind was blowing, a refreshing wind. Reb Hirshele
stood on the deck and contemplated his dilemma. His wife
urged him to put off a decision of any sort until their boat

docked, but he was in the throes of a turbulent inner storm. He feared that he would not be able to withstand the temptation and his weaker side would predominate. "Do not trust yourself until the day you die," warned the Sages. Reb Hirshele strongly felt that now — while he still possessed the moral strength for that action — was the time to destroy the letter.

His wife besought him to wait, but he begged her not to interfere, not to stay his hand. His decision was final. He took out the letter that had been burning a hole in his pocket. Then with a deliberate motion he tore it in half, ripped the halves into shreds and threw them to the winds. The winds sowed the white seeds upon the waves and the waves wafted them up and down. Reb Hirshele's wife looked at her last hope, scattered to the winds and waves, fluttering bravely but only momentarily on the azure crests. So her husband was not destined after all to be acknowledged among the great Torah scholars and rabbis of Jerusalem.

The ship sped away from the white flakes that were soon lost beyond sight and cruised onward, nearing its destination. Soon it would reach the Holy Land, thought Reb Hirshele's wife, where no one would know her husband, no one would realize his great worth, his vast Torah knowledge, his good deeds, his holiness, his humility. The ocean had swallowed them all up together with his prospects.

After several weeks of traveling, Reb Hirshele, his wife and their six children docked in Jaffa and from there they went directly to Jerusalem. On the morrow of their arrival, Reb Hirshele arranged the *chalitza* ceremony in Rav Shmuel Salant's *beith din*.

No one knew what kind of person Reb Hirshele was. While their money lasted, he continued his Torah study privately, devoting night as well as day. When several weeks had gone by and the cash was all depleted, the young children cried out for bread. Reb Hirshele's wife suggested that her husband go to Rav Shmuel and ask to be accepted into the yeshiva. She could not forget the spectacle of the fluttering papers. Alas, she sighed silently, if only we had that letter...

One day passed, another day. The young man realized that his wife was right. The house was bare, and it was time to approach Reb Shmuel and ask to be accepted as a Torah scholar in Etz Chayim. But Reb Hirshele did not wish to put his entire trust in man. He reviewed the words of the *Mesilath Yesharim*, a book he always had in his pocket, that "it was not the endeavor that helped, although endeavor was obligatory." And so, he finally informed his wife, in order to fulfill the obligation of endeavor, he would agree to go to the Rav, but he never-theless thrust his burden, the burden of livelihood, upon God.

To Reb Hirshele's good fortune, no one was in Rav Shmuel's room when he was ushered in. In utter humility, his back bowed and his eyes downcast, Reb Hirshele slow-ly approached the revered figure of the Rav and laid his request before him. "I have no source of income," he gave as his reason for seeking admission to the yeshiva.

Rav Shmuel was astounded, shocked. "Since when does one enter a yeshiva for the income!? Isn't the end purpose of attending a yeshiva to study Torah, to learn and to teach, to immerse oneself wholly in Torah? Once that purpose is perfectly clear then the resources — the bread — will not be lacking." He paused and then continued off-hand, "Well, do you have any letter of recommendation from abroad stating that you are a scholar of some measure, that you are capable of dedicating yourself to Torah study? That you are interested in it?"

Reb Hirshele did not reply. He stood his ground unflinchingly but silently. He could not help remembering the letter from his *rebbi,* the letter he had cast to the wind and sea because he had refused to use Torah as a cutting-axe. Even now, as he stood before the Rav of Jerusalem in shame, he refused to even mention that letter. Half an hour passed thus in silence. The young man maintained his position, his mind far away in the middle of the ocean. Rav Shmuel also made no move; he had meanwhile dozed off in his chair, momentarily relieved of the burden of the flock of the Old City and all the sheep gathered in from the diaspora which rested on his busy, tired shoulders.

Heavy footsteps sounded in the courtyard and the Rav shook himself to alertness. It was the Armenian postman with the day's mail, a huge pile of letters from abroad that had come for the Rav. Reb Hirshele moved back a few steps so as not to disturb Rav Shmuel. The Rav shuffled through the pile in front of him, examining the letters briefly and choosing one from the pack which he opened eagerly. It was from the *Chiddushey haRim* of Gur, and it contained a short note written with wide margins:

My disciple, Reb Hirshele of Tomashov, has immigrated to Jerusalem, the Holy City, may it be speedily rebuilt and restored, and is unknown there. Although I have given him a letter of recommendation to vouch for his qualities, I know him well and fear that he will not deliver that letter to you. Therefore I have rewritten the contents of that first letter of recommendation. The young man in question has been studying Torah through hardship even since he has reached

emotional maturity. He blackens his face laboring
for Torah for its own sake. Please befriend him
and help support him.

"Amazing! Amazing!" Rav Shmuel looked alternately
from the letter to the young man and back to the letter.
Reb Hirshele did not grasp what was going on. He could
not understand why the Rav kept on reading the letter
over and over again, exclaiming in great wonderment.

"You're one of us," The Rav exclaimed feelingly. "You
are one of ours." And he arose to seat the visitor next
to him.

It is quite unnecessary to add that Reb Hirshele was
accepted in the yeshiva that very day and he never stopped
his Torah study until the day he died.

Trachtenberg Regrets

WHEN THE YESHIVA SECRETARY saw the storm of anger in which Asher Trachtenberg had left Rav Shmuel's home, he resolved to at least attempt to mollify the philanthropist. That evening he went to the rich man's hotel to talk to him. It was a difficult task. Mr. Trachtenberg refused to listen. Upon sudden impulse the secretary tried a different approach. He suggested that the philanthropist accompany him to Reb Hirshele's house, where they could peek inside and see what went on. That would give him an inkling of what Rav Shmuel had meant by his praise of the young man.

It was an hour after Ma'ariv.

The secretary found himself a spot by one window and motioned to Mr. Trachtenberg to stand beside him and look inside.

The scene spread before his eyes almost made Mr. Trachtenberg exclaim aloud. The young man was seated at a long table, his naked feet immersed in a basin of cold water to keep him awake, his six children forming a jeweled ring around him. Each boy received two slices of bread with a slice of halvah — a national food — that had been resliced into six slivers. The boys' faces lit up in happiness at the sight of this treat. Reb Hirshele ate his bread without the treat, dipping the dry slices into his tea. When they had all finished eating supper, and thanking God for it, they continued sitting at the table and began to study by the dim light of a kerosene lamp that stood in the center of the table.

Within a short time, a chorus of voices rose and spilled out into the night. Mr. Trachtenberg and the secretary stood outside and watched the scene before them. The rich man's eyes overflowed with tears.

The secretary saw that the visit had worked its magic. He whispered to his guest that the hour was late and it was time for them to return home, but Mr. Trachtenberg refused to leave. The spectacle had so touched him as to break him completely. He stood transfixed by the window looking at the thin faces of the children inside, listening in a trance to their sweet voices raised in study. His eyes would occasionally wander to the father who, nourished by a mouthful of bread and a glass of tea, was able to put such energy and such force into his study. It was something he had never before witnessed.

Two hours passed and the secretary, himself fatigued, reminded the American that it was getting late, high time for him to return to his hotel. But Mr. Trachtenberg persisted; he wanted to look on.

Four hours passed thus in front of the window of Reb Hirshele's humble home. The children fell asleep at the table, one by one, on their open *gemaras*. The father eventually dozed off too. But still, Mr. Trachtenberg would not leave his post.

After another quarter hour had passed, the father suddenly roused himself and gently woke up his children. He brought them water to wash their hands, and again their enthusiastic voices rang out, this time with the Shma prayer. Mr. Trachtenberg finally let himself be led away and back to his hotel room. He had never witnessed such moving, living drama before.

He did not close his eyes all that night. Reb Hirshele's

figure shimmered before his eyes; the sound of his study and the enchanting melody of his children bent over their *gemaras* reverberated in his ears like fine violin music. He could not fall asleep. His thoughts grew introspective; he reflected upon his own deeds, and found his behavior sadly wanting. He had been rude and unmannerly, unappreciative of the young Torah scholar's worth. "The Rav was so right in his censure."

The cock crowed; morning dawned. Mr. Trachtenberg was already at Rav Shmuel's door.

Weeping bitterly, Mr. Trachtenberg begged Rav Shmuel's pardon for his unmannerly behavior, and asked him to prescribe a procedure of *teshuva* for him. Rav Shmuel treated the rich man handsomely, but he referred him to Reb Hirshele himself for a penance and an apology.

Trachtenberg managed to catch Reb Hirshele in the *shul* after Shacharith. Not only did Reb Hirshele gladly "forgive" the American philanthropist, he did not even comprehend what there was to forgive. He had not felt slighted in the least.

At this point, Mr. Trachtenberg suggested that they contract a Yissachar-Zevulun arrangement whereby he would support the Torah scholar in return for a partnership with him in Gan Eiden.

Reb Hirshele would not agree without first consulting his *rebbi* in Gur, the *Chiddushey haRim*, and so the matter rested temporarily.

Asher Trachtenberg left Jerusalem on the morrow, firmly resolving to double and even triple his support to the Old Settlement institutions in the Old City, where such sacred souls resided.

In fact, however, Reb Hirshele was only one of many precious souls who dwelt within the sacred walls of the Holy City of then. There were many Jews of his caliber whose ways were all holiness.

"Sholom Aleichem"

It surely wasn't Reb Daniyel's lot in this world that people envied. What was there to envy in a man who had suffered so many trials and tribulations over the seven-year span since he had left his native Lomza that his hair had turned prematurely white? Was there anything to envy in a man who lived with his seven children in two moldy rooms in a dark, recessed nook?

Did one envy his sons who studied Torah all day and whose sweet voices broke the evening stillness with a captivating beauty? His daughters who excelled in their modesty and piety? These treasures were not such as to arouse an outsider's jealousy, for who in the Jerusalem of then could not boast such treasures of his own? Anyone strolling around the Jewish quarter in the Old City would find every man and woman there instilling Torah values and piety in their children. Where would one find a house from whose depths the sound of Torah did not emanate of a cold winter's eve or hot summer's night? Obviously, anything that Reb Daniyel might have possessed to envy, was also possessed by numerous other families. What, then, was the essence of the envy he aroused?

Rav Yehoshua Leib Diskin's devoted disciples — watching his every motion, his every nuance — had remarked that during the past few monthly blessings of the new moon, the Rav of Brisk would always direct a "Sholom Aleichem" toward Reb Daniyel. Reb Daniyel would usually cringe into one of the corners of the terrace and try to make himself inconspicuous. Rav Yehoshua Leib would nevertheless not desist until he had received an answering "Aleichem Shalom" from that self-effacing young scholar.

Why did this otherwise unsingular person merit such individual attention from the Rav of Brisk, no less? If every shadow of a motion the Rav made was full of significance, what did this singling out mean? No one, not even the great scholars close to the Rav, dared ask. And when one asked Reb Daniyel why he deserved that envied "Shalom Aleichem," he himself had no answer to offer. It wasn't that he was evading them or trying to hide something. He honestly did not know!

In any case, the Rav's disciples treated Reb Daniyel with respect. As for Reb Daniyel, he might easily have lived out the eighty-odd years allotted him without anyone ever discovering the reason behind the coveted "Shalom Aleichem," were it not for his wife, Ethel, through whose mouth the story inadvertently found its way out. Truthfully, though, it never became fully certain that this story was what had so impressed the Rav of Brisk.

Ethel had been charged with a stringent command by her father, Reb Yudel Bialystoker, as he lay on his deathbed. Two days before his death, the old man had expressed the brief message that was his last will and testament, "Be of assistance to your husband so that he need never, God forbid, waste even one hour of Torah study or prayer because of you."

Ethel, then in her first year of marriage, had faithfully heeded her father's last words. Her constant worry was that her husband never miss any of his regular study sessions. Her neighbors used to relate that she never sent her husband to the market for any purchase whatsoever. Nor did she ever ask him to help her in any household task that would take him away from his studies. Reb Daniyel's foot never stepped into a Jerusalem market; he never spoke to a druggist across the counter, never once addressed a storekeeper. Righteous Ethel preferred to do all these tasks herself rather than waste a precious minute of her husband's learning time. She maintained the household and kept it running smoothly, solely by her own efforts. This was her whole purpose in life, her *raison d'être*.

It happened, however, that one Thursday Reb Daniyel was seen wandering through the marketplaces of the Old City with a huge sack slung over his head. *Whatever is he doing in the Batrak shuk*? everyone wondered. No one had the audacity to ask. They did not want to hurt his feelings.

When Reb Daniyel returned from the marketplace that Thursday evening, his wife felt obligated to explain to at least one neighbor why she had let her husband deviate from his principle.

Entering the home of her neighbor, Chaya Schwartz, she told her the whole story. "Believe me," she justified herself and her Daniyel, "my husband has not undergone any sudden transformation. Nor have I changed my ways. Rather, this is what happened.

"Yesterday, while my husband was studying, a Yemeni old-clothing peddler passed our doorway advertising his wares. *'Alte zachen,'* he called out loudly. 'Old clothing for sale.' I went outside to examine whether he had among his wares anything suitable for my children. Going through his pile, I set aside a small bundle of things I could use. At that moment my husband, who had been deeply immersed in his study, came out to whisper in my ear that I had better check the clothing for *shaatnez* before I purchased anything. Asking the peddler to wait a moment, I quickly selected two or three coats from the pile and took them to Reb Shmuel Zavil, the *shaatnez* expert, who, after inspecting them over, found them all to contain the forbidden mixture of wool and linen. I returned the coats to the peddler without purchasing anything and he continued on his way. My husband meanwhile went on to the yeshiva and he returned late that evening.

"Next morning my husband suddenly remembered the incident and asked what had happened with the clothes. When he heard my account, he turned pale and began trembling. 'What?!' he exclaimed fearfully, 'We must find out immediately where that Yemeni peddler lives. Who knows if some Jew has not already stumbled and transgressed the strict prohibition of *shaatnez*!'

"I inquired among all my neighbors about the peddler and after much running back and forth I finally tracked the man down. He lived in some spot in the Batrak market in a room that was half cellar, half living-quarters. My husband immediately gathered all the money we owned and even went to borrow some from the neighbors after which he ran right to the peddler's home and interrogated him about his wares. The man pointed to a large pile of old clothing in a corner of the cellar and my husband went out to acquire a large sack. When he returned, he made a deal with the peddler, bought out his entire stock, and brought the sackful of old clothing home. There he prepared a roaring bonfire and joyfully threw the sack with its contents into the blaze. 'Now no Jerusalem Jew can unwittingly be trapped into buying *shaatnez*.'"

Reb Zev Schwartz heard this story from his wife and told it to the Rav of Brisk. At that time, the Rav did not react visibly to the story. But his close disciples assumed that this had raised Reb Daniyel's stock in the Rav's eyes.

Litvak Becomes Chassid

REB DANIYEL WAS of sound mind but of weak constitution. In those times, eye diseases were rampant in Jerusalem and the stern arm of heavenly justice struck the *tzaddik* with a severe eye affliction. At first he tried to alleviate his pain with *Tehillim* and prayers, and his friends also prayed for his recovery. But the disease worsened and Reb Daniyel's doctors prescribed a whole month of enforced darkness to rest his eyes.

When a month had passed over Reb Daniyel's bandaged eyes and shuttered house, the sun was once again allowed to enter his life. However, the warm rays did not shed any light upon the afflicted eyes. Day followed day and his condition grew increasingly worse. For two years the *tzaddik* had been suffering, his sight nearly gone and the pain excruciating. Reb Daniyel's doctors forbade him to study any text whatsoever — and that hurt most, for what was life worth if he could not study his precious Torah?

Indeed, he could not withstand this trial.

His good wife Ethel was filled with sorrow. Whenever she lit Shabbath candles she poured out a sea of tears to her Father in heaven and prayed on behalf of her husband that his eyes would not be darkened forever.

"Eyes that labored so much over the Torah and never gazed at forbidden sights, eyes that shed countless tears over the sorrow of the Divine Presence — please let these eyes be illuminated again that they may continue to enjoy the light of Your Torah."

Finding that the medication did not help him anyway, Reb Daniyel had given up on his doctors and refused to obey their instructions. Ignoring his own physical short-comings, he continued his studies throughout the day and into part of the night. Naturally, his eyes grew worse and he was often forced to close his book in the midst of his study. He would weep whenever this happened, sometimes wailing like a baby. A cry would escape his lips, "Uncover my eyes that I may witness the wonders of your Torah."

King David may have spoken figuratively, but Reb Daniyel meant the words of the psalm literally. "Uncover my eyes, uncover my eyes," he prayed. And his prayers, together with his wife's, went up to heaven.

On the first day of Rosh HaShana, during the customary *tashlich* ceremony, Ethel met the wife of Rav El'azar Mendel Biderman of Lelov, whose father had led thousands of chassidim in Europe but had given up that glory to settle in Jerusalem. The rebbetzin, a righteous woman on her own account, greeted Ethel respectfully and, after reciting the *tashlich* prayer, asked her politely about her health. Ethel found this an opportune moment to pour out her troubles to the good woman.

The rebbetzin tried to comfort the unhappy Ethel and promised to ask her husband to beg for heavenly mercy for Reb Daniyel.

Ethel's troubled heart struck a responsive chord in the rebbetzin and she kept her promise faithfully. When she returned home she entered her husband's study, and told him that Reb Daniyel was suffering severe eye trouble. She begged him to pray for that worthy man's speedy and complete recovery. Her husband did not interrupt his thoughts, but nodded to indicate that he had heard her.

When Rosh haShana was over, Rav El'azar sent his
son, Reb Davidl, who later succeeded him as head of the
Lelover chassidim in Jerusalem, to Reb Daniyel with
a copy of *Me'or Eynayim*, written by Rav Menachem
Nachum of Tchernobl, a disciple of the Baal Shem Tov.
He had him tell Reb Daniyel to study the *seifer* carefully,
continually, with the promise that if he did, his eyes
would regain their sight.

Reb Daniyel was descended from the disciples of the
Gaon of Vilna. His family were devout *mithnagdim*, opponents of the chassidim. He therefore hesitated at first to
peruse a volume so thoroughly chassidic, but his wife, who
came from solid chassidic stock, did not relent from her
entreaties until he finally agreed. Every day Reb Daniyel
would sit and study *Me'or Eynayim* for half an hour. To
his great surprise and the surprise of his near ones, his
eyes slowly began to heal and regain their former powers.

Although Reb Daniyel did not become a full-fledged
chassid, and when he said *kaddish* he still omitted the
words *Veyatzmach purkoneih vikoreiv meshicheih*, he
did become a fervent chassid of Reb El'azar Mendel, and
the *seifer* the *rebbe* gave him never left his table.

The Grocery Store

REB DANIYEL'S TWIN BROTHER, Reb Sheima, had succeeded in immigrating to Jerusalem three years before his brother. He earned his livelihood from a tiny grocery store that nested in one of the nooks of the Misgav Ladach Hospital building in the Old City. The thirty-two-year-old grocer had spent an entire year of holy service under Rav Yisrael Lipkin of Salant, founder of the mussar movement. Under his pious tutelage, Reb Sheima had learned how severe were the prohibitions against stealing, cheating, and deception. Ever since, he had kept a healthy distance from ill-gotten or ill-earned money, even if it involved only a doubt of transgression.

Reb Sheima never let anyone sell his merchandise to the customers, not even his wife. He simply was afraid that no one would weigh out the measures as exactly as he did. Even his chronic lung disease did not prevent Reb Sheima from serving his customers personally so that he could give them the benefit of the doubt in weights and measures. Each week he would check his scale and his weights in the pharmacy for fear that they might have been rubbed off somewhat and lost weight in the process, in which case he would be cheating his customers. This sin, he knew, was one that not even Yom Kippur nor the sacrifice of a herd of rams could erase.

Reb Sheima's customers witnessed his amazing exactness in his business practices. If, for example, a customer would request, "Good herring, please," Reb Shaima would reply, "I've got a herring for you but I don't know if it is a good one." If a child came to buy sweets or such, he would send him back home to get a note of permission. The *cheider* children knew that you didn't enter Reb Sheima's grocery store for candles without a note from home. And if a steady customer of another storekeeper should wish to purchase something from him, Reb Sheima would send the prospective customer away empty-handed.

Despite all the credit due him, Reb Sheima did not refrain from asking numerous halachic questions, even when the answers meant a reduction in business and income. Second and third degree doubts robbed him of peace of mind until such time as he could go to a Rav for a halachic decision. Only when Reb Shaima had heard the decision in the clearest of language, devoid of any ambiguities, was his equanimity restored — until the next doubt arose.

Reb Sheima devoutly wished that the Rav of Brisk would deign to answer his problems on a regular basis. However, since he himself did not dare enter to present his own questions — he still remembered with what trembling and awe his *rebbi,* the great Rav Yisrael of Salant, would mention the name of that holy personality — he sought a different solution.

What did he do? He found himself a go-between. Rav Zarach Braverman was close enough to the Rav of Brisk to present halachic problems to him without flinching. And Reb Sheima did not feel the same overpowering awe for Rav Zarach as he did for Rav Yehoshua Leib Diskin. And so, whenever a question arose, the humble grocer would approach the good Torah scholar, begging him to present the question to the *tzaddik* and to bring him back a clear decision. Rav Zarach, for his part, knew Reb

Sheima to be a truly pious Jew with a highly-developed fear of sin, and could not refuse his requests. Rav Zarach would enter the Rav's study with the question, receive an answer on the spot, and relay it to the waiting Reb Sheima. When he had his answer, Reb Sheima would heave a sigh of relief and become a new man. Rav Zarach could see that the Rav of Brisk enjoyed these questions, deriving great satisfaction from the fact that a shopkeeper should be so exacting in business practices.

And what, for example, were Reb Sheima's questions?

The Talmud states that one may not mix prime quality fruits with poorer quality produce. What should the poor grocer do if the wholesaler supplies him with a mixture of qualities? Might he sell the fruits as he had bought them, or was he obligated to separate them first before selling them?

Another problem that bothered Reb Sheima was that of Chol Hamo'ed sales. Reb Sheima only kept the store open during Chol Hamo'ed because he needed the income for his day-to-day expenses. That was permissible. The pious grocer wanted to know, however, if he must close the main entrance to the store, the one that faced the street, and make his customers enter from the door that led through his house, or if he might keep the outer door open even on Chol Hamo'ed so that his customers would not think that the store was closed.

An Explanation in the "Chinnuch"

REB SHEIMA once sent Rav Zarach to the Rav of Brisk with a difficult problem. Upon testing his weights, Reb Sheima had found one of them wanting. The discrepancy was minute, but it nevertheless deeply disturbed the honest shopkeeper. His question was: since he checked his weights regularly from week to week, could he assume that the change in its accuracy had occured just before this week's test? Or did he have to reimburse all the customers who had made purchases from him throughout the entire week?

Rav Zarach would sometimes ask lengthy questions, sometimes brief ones. But the Rav always gave short, succinct answers.

This time the rebbetzin happened to hear the question. Known for her sharpness, her quickwittedness, and her strict adherence to the Halachah, the rebbetzin had been listening alertly while salting her meat in the kitchen. When Rav Zarach emerged from the house with his reply in hand, she called out to him,

"Remind Reb Sheima to get rid of the faulty weight immediately. It is forbidden to keep faulty weights in one's house."

Reb Sheima heard her speaking, but could not discern her words. As Rav Zarach approached, he asked what the rebbetzin had found so important to call out to him. "Don't be upset," Rav Zarach reassured the worried storekeeper. "She only observed that you may not leave the faulty weight lying around your house."

"Truly," Reb Sheima recollected, "when I brought that weight home from the store, my wife wanted to use it to pulverize olives. But when my ten-year-old Shloimele came home from *cheider* and say his mother using the stone, he shouted out, 'Mother, I learned in *cheider* that you mustn't keep that in the house.' He would not rest until he had thrown the weight with his own hands into the dustbin. His mother then went over and kissed him on the forehead."

Reb Sheima and Rav Zarach, walking homeward, discussing the Rav's decision and its practical application, had not gotten far before the *Rav* called his *shamash*, Reb Nota, and bade him summon the poser of the question.

Reb Nota understood this to mean Reb Sheima himself, and he went to deliver the message to him. He ran after the two men and caught up with them when they were already past the Batey Machseh square. Speaking directly to Reb Sheima he said, "The Rav wants you."

"Who? Me? The Rav? Me?" asked the bewildered Reb Sheima.

Greater people than Reb Sheima were seized with uncontrollable trembling in the Rav's presence. Reb Sheima entered dripping from a cold sweat. It was the first time he stood before the awe-inspiring figure of the Rav of Brisk, and he had been summoned! His knees knocking, his figure bent forward in homage, his eyes downcast for fear of being blinded by the radiance, he tried to control himself so that he could listen with all his faculties.

"You asked a question today about weights," the Rav began. "I merely wished to add that the *Seifer haChinnuch* states the opinion that even the slightest aberration in weights and measures is forbidden."

White as chalk, Reb Sheima left the Rav's house and returned home with ringing ears. The few words echoed and reechoed in them.

Was it merely to tell me this opinion cited by the Chinnuch *that the Rav had me summoned?* Reb Sheima asked himself over and over, all through the night. He could not fall asleep for the great emotional upheaval he had undergone in the short interview. Did the Rav's words have any other deep significance? If so, what was it?

"Well, why didn't you ask the Rav what he meant right away?" his wife Devora demanded. "If you were inside already, couldn't you take the opportunity to speak a few words to him?"

"Oy, Devora," he moaned, "you don't even begin to understand what it is to talk to the Brisker Rav. What can a woman know of these matters, anyway!"

The words continued to ring in his mind, phrases and words in the Rav's tones. Awake and asleep, the words danced before Reb Sheima's eyes, "Opinion. . . *Chinnuch*. . . forbidden. . ."

"Reb Sheima!" Rav Eli'ezer Dan Ralbag scolded the naive shopkeeper for his overworked imagination, "All the Rav said was that according to the *Chinnuch*'s opinion, even a minute aberration in weight is forbidden. That's all. The words were meant to be understood at their face value and no more. Why do you have to invent hints and hidden significances?"

"But," Reb Sheima tried to justify himself, "isn't there always a hidden explanation of the text following the simple one?"

214

The Leader of the Generation Settles
in Jerusalem

WHAT KIND OF PEOPLE came to live in Jerusalem? What type of man left his homeland, his birthplace, and his family to go and settle desolate Mount Zion? Who was able to turn his back on the wealth of the diaspora in exchange for the dark alleys of the abandoned city?

To begin with, there were the ascetics, the Perushim, people lovesick for the Divine Presence who had concluded their business with this world. Such people chose to die in the tents of Torah, letting their bodies subsist on the meager ration of bread and water for which the monthly allotment they received from the yeshiva sufficed.

Although these people were the elite of Jerusalem's settlers, they were not its leaders. Leadership demanded different sacrifices. It required throwing behind oneself a career of Torah-leadership, of propagating Torah, of communal development in the diaspora, and leaving one's flocks without a shepherd, one's city without a guide.

Among the few such figures was the giant from Brisk, Rav Yehoshua Leib Diskin. He was a true leader, for in assuming the leadership of Jerusalem, he left behind him the rabbinate of a flowering community, the teaching of hundreds of *talmidim,* and the guidance of all of diaspora Jewry.

Between the time the news of his decision to come to Eretz Yisrael arrived until he actually settled in Jerusalem, Jerusalem Jewry made many conjectures as to what the Rav proposed to do within the divine city.

"He will surely establish a huge yeshiva to which hundreds of *talmidim* will flock from all over the world," was one opinion.

"Maybe he will have the peace of mind to enable him to write thousands of responsa to Jews throughout the exile."

Other surmises pointed to a different direction. "Maybe he is only coming to visit the holy sites, pray there, and then return to Brisk."

When Rav Yehoshua Leib decided to dwell in Jerusalem, it was not because he thought that the city lacked Torah. He knew that the holy city did not need another yeshiva. But he did feel the ominous, black cloud that was darkening the skies of the Holy Land. He renounced all his glory in the diaspora and went to save the Jewish settlement which was being renewed in Eretz Yisrael — to save it from impending danger.

Jerusalem Jewry was not aware of the coming danger. The perceptive citizens of the Old Settlement did, however, comment on the fact that at the ceremony in his welcome, the Rav of Brisk addressed himself to the young *cheider* pupils who had come to pay him homage. "There must be something to it," people said.

What was the danger threatening the Holy Land? What was it that caused the leader of the diaspora to leave his abundant flock and dedicate his efforts and talents to Eretz Yisrael?

The progressives, the modern Jews, the *maskilim,* as they were known, had been trying for dozens of years to get a foothold in Jerusalem in particular and in Eretz Yisrael in general. Their burning aim was to spread a net which would entrap Jewish youth. Danger threatened

216

everywhere. Poverty and scarcity were on the progressives' side, adding weight to their offers of free milk, warm meals, and suitable clothing to the emaciated children of so many helpless parents. But even with these lures they did not succeed in their activities. Jerusalem's Torah-true Jews were not taken in; they refused to be ensnared by their free-thinking, Torah-denying brothers. They gave those atheists a wide berth.

At the time that the Rav of Brisk made his move to the Holy City, the *maskilim,* sensing failure, were in the midst of changing their tactics. The men they were then beginning to send to Jerusalem to hunt souls bore the outward trappings of orthodox Jews and could quote talmudic sources for their purposes.

Rav Yehoshua Leib was aware of this. And this is what prodded him to join his unsuspecting brothers and protect them. He settled in a tiny apartment in the Old City but his net was cast all over the Holy Land. Shortly after his arrival, his efforts were evident in the field of education.

About two months after the giant of Brisk's resettlement, a dawn arrival aroused the curiosity of his neighbors. For one thing, the carriage that rolled up and screeched to a halt in front of the Rav's door had come all the way from Hebron, which it must have left in the darkness of the night in order to arrive here at dawn. That alone, however, did not necessarily signify anything extraordinary; conceivably — as some neighbors guessed — special messengers had been sent to beg for the Rav's last-minute prayers for someone on his deathbed. But this theory was quickly quashed when out of the carriage stepped the Rav of Hebron, 100-year-old Rav Shimon Menashe Chaikin, accompanied by a communal figure of that city.

What pressing business could drive the centenarian out of the comfort of bed and home in the midst of the night?

No one knew. Why did he have to come to the Rav of Brisk just as morning was dawning? Only one citizen of Jerusalem besides the Rav himself had an idea, and that was Rav Yaakov Orenstein, who happened to be at the Rav's when the distinguished guest arrived. As he accompanied the Hebron sage back to his carriage after the meeting with the Rav of Brisk, he learned the facts of the story.

An Indian Jew named Yochanan Benvenishti had visited Hebron two weeks before, Rav Shimon Menashe told Rav Yaakov. The man was known for his vast wealth and for his connections in government circles. He was influenced by *maskilim* to found a secular school in Hebron for the Oriental Jews who comprised the majority of the city's population. The danger was imminent and ominous.

"Just yesterday," continued the Rav of Hebron, "I convened with these would-be founders in a final attempt to deter them. Seeing that my efforts were all in vain, I hurried to discuss the next step with your master, the giant of this generation."

"And what did the Rav say to you?" Rav Yaakov asked curiously.

"He promised me that the school would not be established."

"Amazing!"

The marvel was all the more pronounced when after several weeks the news reached Jerusalem that the new school was a forgotten project; the plans for it had been entirely abandoned. What had gone on behind the scenes remained a dark secret, however, for who had the audacity to poke a curious head in matters that were above him and concerned the Torah giants?

From India to Jerusalem

In 5652 (1892), a year after the demise of the Brisker Rav, a delegation of rabbis from Budapest came to visit Rav Yosef Chayim Sonnenfeld. Among other things they discussed the Brisker Rav's greatness. Every one of the rabbis had something to say on this popular subject. Rav Yosef Chayim listened to their stories and observations with interest. "Great are the deeds of *tzaddikim*," everyone agreed. Then it was Rav Chayim's turn. "Let me tell you a short but unusual narrative about my teacher and *rebbi*, an incident that will reveal a sample of the extent of his greatness.

"In 5637, when the Rav was en route to Jerusalem to settle, he was forced to spend a week in Paris to arrange certain official papers. Very few people in Paris had heard of the *tzaddik*, and the Rav was glad of this. He rented a room on the outskirts of the city, far from the urban noise and tumult. This room neighbored on a small *beith midrash* frequented by twenty-odd older men who lived nearby.

"The Rav used this *beith midrash* as his day time headquarters, sitting all day deep in study and prayer, crowned by his *tefillin* and enveloped in his *tallith*.

"One afternoon, while he was studying alone, an Oriental Jew suddenly entered, dressed in the manner of noblemen. He ran over to the Rav, bowed and, grabbing hold of his hand, kissed it reverently and began crying bitterly.

219

The Rav tried to calm the distraught man but he fell down in a faint. The Rav tried to rouse him. He filled a ewer with water and poured its contents on the man's face. When the man had regained consciousness, the Rav spoke to him kindly,

" 'What is the matter, fellow-Jew? Tell me what is troubling your heart and you will find relief. With God's help I may even be able to assist you.'

"Like dew on a parched flower, the words effected visible signs of relief on the stranger. 'My name is Sasson Ben-venishti and I was born in Calcutta, India. Although the members of my family have lived in India among the heathens for the past seven generations, we have nevertheless not forgotten our tradition. We observe the Torah and its mitzvoth with fervent devotion. I am prodigiously wealthy and own vast properties in India and other countries and so I have, thank God, never known want or suffering. But my good days are all over now. For the past two years I have been afflicted with a severe lung disease which my physicians say will not give me much longer to live. My family in Bombay forced me to consult the famous physician here known as De Paris, who is an expert in pulmonary disease. With not much hope in my heart, I came to Paris to seek this doctor's advice. At my consultation this morning, the doctor informed me that my only hope was to undergo a serious and risky operation. He said that since the chances of success were slim, he left the decision entirely up to me but if I were to agree he would undertake the operation next Sunday.'

"In tearful tones, the Indian Jew continued to speak. He related how an Ashkenazic rabbi whom he knew had informed him that a great Lithuanian *tzaddik* was in Paris and might be able to help or advise him.

"Overcome by physical and mental anguish at this point, the foreigner fell at the Rav's feet, 'Rabbi, holy rabbi, bless me! Give me an amulet; let me give a redemption donation; whisper some charm over me. Do something for my suffering, O holy man! Pray for me and save me. I promise to increase my public activities twofold, fourfold. I will support Torah scholars; I will uphold Torah institutions...'

"The Rav did not give him an amulet; he did not prescribe a *pidyon*. Nor did he chant any charms over him, nor did he make him promise any promises. In his usual curt manner, the Rav spoke clearly and concisely. 'Don't visit any more doctors. You do not need an operation at all. Your pain will gradually subside and I assure you that you will live long.' As a matter of fact, Benvenishti lived to one hundred.

"When the nobleman heard these words his eyes lit up. The Rav's promise of a speedy recovery without an operation restored his serenity and happiness. He thanked the Rav profusely and returned to the lavish hotel where his wife and children awaited him. However, when he related his experience with the Lithuanian rabbi, he was interrupted by his wife's angry reaction. 'Can it be?' she doubted. 'Can a rabbi who spends the entire day in study halls, divorced from worldly matters and untutored in medicine, can such a person accept upon himself the responsibility of so weighty a decision in defiance of a professional opinion from a world-famous surgeon?'

"The man's oldest son, Yochanan, spoke up in support of his mother's argument. 'See, the king of Austria who recently suffered from the identical disease that you have, was operated upon by this very doctor and is now well and healthy.' At this point the wife began to weep, begging her husband to have pity on his family and to agree to

221

undergo surgery. Benvenishti was swayed by such insistent pleas and finally agreed to the operation. When he entered the hospital on the day scheduled, the surgeon had everything prepared and the patient was even brought to the operating table. But at the last moment the famous physician expressed regret: His latest examination showed that the operation would be too great a risk. The Jew was removed from the table and sent home, with the physician's regret that he had no alternate cure for him. 'But you are a Jew, are you not?' De Paris said in parting. 'Pray to your omnipotent God; He can still help you.'

"These parting words stabbed the Jew cruelly, for they recalled to him the Rav's advice that he had so readily abandoned. His family was also visited by compunction and remorse at the doubt they had all displayed in the Rav's advice. Clearly he had had some prescience in the matter. They hired a carriage and rushed to the *beith midrash* where the Rav of Brisk spent his days in study. Upon entering they fell at his feet, weeping loudly. They begged forgiveness for their doubts and besought his help.

"Benvenishti arose and handed the Rav a jeweled box, decorated with rare diamonds. It contained gold coins which the nobleman was giving to the Rav as a gift. Without even looking at the box or its contents, the Rav assured the donor and his family that he had not the slightest intention of accepting a gift. He never accepted any gifts, he informed them. Benvenishti took this as a personal insult and almost fainted again from the affront. Once again the Rav calmed the emotional Oriental Jew and explained that he never had and never would accept gifts and he surely did not mean to hurt the generous donor. He once again outlined his instructions: the Indian was to keep his distance from doctors, return home, and await God's imminent succor.

" 'The day may yet come when I will require your services,' the Rav pronounced prophetically.

" 'I will forever be at your service. I will never forget the kindness you have done me,' the Indian promised.

"This time the family took their leave with full confidence in the Rav's instructions. They embarked that very day for their home in India. Several days later the Rav of Brisk himself set sail for his new home in Jerusalem.

"Although many events filled the interval between the incident in Paris and the visit from the Rav of Hebron, the Rav of Brisk did not forget. And when Rav Shimon Menashe appeared with his forecast of impending doom for Jewish education in the city of Hebron, Rav Yehoshua Leib heard the name Benvenishti and trembled. Inquiring about the man's origin and identity, he knew that the battle was already won. He was able to assure the old rabbi at once that the school would not be established. And after the Rav of Hebron left, the Rav sat down at his desk and took pen in hand. The letter he wrote was addressed to Sasson Benvenishti, Calcutta, India.

> My good friend Sasson,
>
> I hereby wish to remind you of your promise of half a year ago in the little Parisian *beith midrash*. I request you to warn your son, Yochanan, in severe terms, to abandon his plans of establishing a school in Hebron. Let him not be led astray by deceivers.
>
> *Yehoshua Leib Diskin of Brisk*

"When the letter arrived at its destination, Benvenishti's heart leaped into his throat as he read the signature. He owed his life to the Rav of Brisk; indeed, he had enjoyed a remarkable improvement in health, much to the amazement of all his doctors. Now he was being called on to repay the favor. He well remembered the Rav's adamant refusal to accept any gift at the time, how the great man

223

had firmly pushed aside a huge fortune. And now, deeply in the Rav's debt already, his own son was causing the great *tzaddik* aggravation. Benvenishti immediately went to his son's house and warned him explicitly to cease and desist from the activities that were grieving the Rav of Brisk.

"Yochanan heard his father's words with surprise written all over his face. His father then produced the letter he had just received. Even then, Yochanan could not understand what connection the Lithuanian Rav had with establishing a school. How could a program of languages and science thwart or anger the *tzaddik* from Brisk? But then he remembered his own reluctance to heed the Rav's words when his father had first relayed them, and how they had all subsequently been convinced that the Divine will was being expressed through that wise man's throat. And so he pulled out his files on the school — the building plans, the teacher contracts, everything — and ripped them up with one grand flourish, right before his father's eyes. And the Jews of Hebron were able to breathe freely."

Only then did Jerusalem begin to understand why the Rav of Brisk had dedicated a special message to the young ears of the *cheider* boys in his first public appearance. He had demonstrated his position as their patron and trustworthy guardian from that day on.

ירושלים של מעלה

Hidden Tzaddikim
in Jerusalem
of Old

Eulogy for an Unknown Soul

WRAPPED UP IN HIS *tallith*, Reb Nota Weiss, the famous Maggid of Jerusalem, stood for three quarters of an hour before the congregation at the Rabban Yochanan ben Zakkai synagogue and eulogized a man named Reb Godl who had been buried in Peki'in in the upper Galilee.

Outside of those bare facts, it seemed that few had known the man or even heard of him. It even seemed to his audience as if Reb Nota himself had not known the deceased. Why then was Reb Nota calling attention to this man on this seventh day of Adar?

Actually it was Rav Shmuel Salant, Rav of Jerusalem, who had put the Maggid up to it. Summoning him that afternoon, the Rav had informed Reb Nota that a certain Jew, a tailor called Reb Godl, had just passed away in Peki'in. Fearing that he would not be properly eulogized in that faraway place, Rav Shmuel had directed Reb Nota to hold his address in the Rabban Yochanan ben Zakkai synagogue between *mincha* and *ma'ariv*. "If I had the strength," added the old Rav, "I would attend myself."

"What should I say about the deceased?" Reb Nota wanted to know.

"Tell your audience that very fact. That if I had the strength, I would myself attend the *hesped*."

Not much time remained to call together a crowd, but the word passed from mouth to ear.

It is possible that among the older people who came

to the *hesped*, there were some who remembered Reb Godl from the time he had resided in Jerusalem. But even those few probably could not see why his death should be of moment, why a simple tailor — that was how they remembered him — should deserve public mourning. They might have even thought to themselves that simply because he had not known the deceased personally, Reb Nota was able to shed tears over him. Had he known Reb Godl...

But of course no one dared express such thoughts aloud. Everyone understood that if the Rav had ordered a *hesped*, he knew what he was doing.

The *hesped* ended and the assembly *davvened ma'ariv*. They dispersed, and the incident was forgotten as are most incidents forgotten in the course of time.

Why then did Rav Shmuel see fit to eulogize the tailor?

Actually not much was known about Reb Godl. His life was a closed chapter in which only several incidental facts were known or remembered by Jerusalem's elders.

When he was still a young man he had owned a tailor shop. A small room served Reb Godl as a shop during the day and as living quarters at night. Facing the Rabban Yochanan ben Zakkai synagogue, the little store boasted a modest sign that read in Rashi print, שנײַדער — TAILOR. Most of the day the shop was closed, and during the hour and a half that it was open, it did not do a flourishing business.

Reb Godl was an idiosyncratic person, silent, strange, removed. But for all this his face always glowed with good nature; his eyes always shone. The tailor *davvened* daily in the tradesmen's synagogue. He had a lazy, careless air about him.

If the truth must be said, there were several Yerushal-mim who suspected him of being a *nistar*, a secretly exalted Jew. But no one was ever able to actually catch him at

228

supernatural practices. Reb Godl somehow managed to camouflage all his deeds in an aura of mystery and obscurity.

If one asked him, for example, why he was so silent, he would gently reply, "God created man with two watch-guards over his mouth, his teeth and his lips. Since all but one of my teeth have fallen out and I am left with one guard of the two, I have to watch my mouth twice as carefully so that I don't sin in speech."

Sometimes people would see him running through the Jerusalem streets. "Where are you rushing to?" they would ask him. "I'm a tradesman and my time is precious," he would reply curtly.

Questioned why his store was hardly ever open, he would retort, "When my door is closed, I am able to get my work done inside."

When his butcher would ask Reb Godl how a family of six could subsist on the tiny measure of meat that he bought each week he would answer sharply, "Do you think that you are the only butcher in Jerusalem?" The butcher, who knew well enough that his customer did not patronize any other store, would be silenced.

Reb Godl would give the same reply to his milkman, to his grocer, and to the other tradesmen. Such obscure statements did not lend themselves to pinpointing greatness.

It happened one time, however, that Reb Godl was almost caught, and his secret almost revealed...

The Shinover Tzaddik Visits Jerusalem

JERUSALEM BUBBLED WITH ACTIVITY, burned with enthusiasm. The city was being honored with a great man's presence; the Shinover Rebbe, son of the *Divrey Chayim* of Tzanz, was coming to visit the Jerusalem of 5631. Not for many years had such a personality, a leader of tens of thousands of Jews, graced the Holy City.

There were several theories as to why the *tzaddik* had decided to spend a whole year in Jerusalem, away from his empire of chassidim in Europe. Rumor had it that he had come on a mysterious mission from his holy father. The only soul who knew for sure was Rav El'azar Mendel Biderman, who visited the *tzaddik* daily and shared his confidence.

Jerusalem, a city whose very essence was holiness, reacted strongly to this personality — a lion the son of a lion — who had come to its midst. Yerushalmim outdid themselves in paying homage to the celebrity. Old and young attired themselves in holiday garb and went forth to greet the *tzaddik*. No announcements were made, no notices posted on walls of public places. Even so, the crowds were prodigious. One word from the mouth of Rav El'azar Mendel Biderman about the visitor's greatness was sufficient to get all the Yerushalmim out of their homes.

The *tzaddik* entered the walls of the city of holiness, the city of the *Mikdash*, riding on his donkey, his eyes burn-

ing with a holy fire. He was greeted by the faces of un-
familiar Jews invested with holy spirit and purity, the legions
of the King of kings, who faithfully guarded the sacredness
of His city even in its destruction and desolation. These
loyal soldiers lined both sides of the narrow, covered
streets. Joy and excitement flushed the faces of all
Jerusalem Jewry.

The crowning event of the day was when Rav El'azar
Mendel Biderman appeared at the head of the huge
crowd. He had never appeared so publicly before.

One or two days passed and the excitement subsided.
The Rebbe of Shinov became the house guest of Rav
El'azar Mendel. The pair would be seen each night venturing forth outside the city wall, and advancing with
deliberate steps toward Har haZeithim, all the while
deeply immersed in their whispered secrets which ordinary
mortals did not venture to guess at. The inhabitants of
Jerusalem only dared to peek at them through the cracks
in the wall, their hearts bursting with emotion at the sight
of those two heavenly angels surrounding the walls of
Jerusalem with a mystery of holiness.

Suddenly, someone threw a bombshell. Berel the blacksmith, who was an expert in all the latest news, related
that one night, just before midnight, the holy pair was
seen walking toward the grave of Shimon haTzaddik with
Reb Godl in tow!

Someone else recalled that he, too, had seen the two
tzaddikim headed for that holy site, again engrossed in a
conversation with the tailor.

It is easy to imagine what a stir that bit of news caused.
The question now arose in all its fury! Was Reb Godl
truly a great man, or had he attached himself to the holy
pair without their permission?

It turned out that when the Shinover Rebbe had requested that Rav El'azar Mendel provide him with a personal *shamash* for the nighttime, the latter suggested Reb Godl for the job. And he served in this capacity for the entire year of the *tzaddik's* stay. He was thus seen night after night entering the Rebbe's inner sanctum.

This fact alone turned Reb Godl into somewhat of a celebrity, and the whispers that had surrounded his person acquired more substance. This publicity depressed the tailor, who sought some way to escape public notice. But nothing helped.

When the Shinover *tzaddik* returned home and the Yerushalmim heard that he had told his father that he had discovered one of the thirty-six *tzaddikim* in whose merit the world exists, they were almost convinced that he was referring to Reb Godl.

In order to still some of the rumors, Reb Godl tried keeping his store open for longer hours, but this didn't stop those who were determined to talk.

The preceding might have been forgotten in the course of the years and Reb Godl might have reverted to being thought of as a simple tailor once more. But one other incident ripped away his camouflage completely. Rav Eliyahu Mani, the Chacham of Hebron, a great *mekubal*, came during the week of *selichoth* to *davven* at the Kothel haMaaravi. On his way home, this great man stopped off to pay a visit to Reb Godl at his shop. After this revealing incident, Reb Godl was unable to maintain his guise any longer. Distressed by all the publicity, Reb Godl left the city on the very next day together with his family for Peki'in. There he spent his remaining thirty years as a "simple" tailor...

On very rare occasions he was seen in Jerusalem. When the Rav of Brisk convened an assembly of all the great Torah scholars to renew the ban on secular schools in Jerusalem, it is said that Reb Godl attended. And on the bitter, tragic day of Rav Yehoshua Leib Diskin's funeral, he was among the pallbearers.

Of Peki'in's mere sixty Jews, probably not one of them recognized the true worth of the tailor who came to settle in their midst. But they were aware of one unusual thing: upon his grave in Peki'in the members of the Chevra Kadisha placed a large round stone that bore the inscription, "This stone rested each night under the head of the deceased, Reb Godl, may he rest in peace, who is buried here."

And by the way, when Rav Shimon Hausman, the great scholar from Hebron who accompanied the Shinover Rebbe on many of his trips, heard of Reb Godl's death, he ripped his clothing in mourning.

These hints illuminate the words of Jerusalem's Rav, "If I had the strength, I would attend the *hesped* myself."

Mistaken Burial

IT WAS A STORMY *motza'ey* Asara beTeiveith night. The Old City was covered with a snowy white blanket. Lightning and thunder declared war upon the rooftops while a fierce wind blew out street lamps on the deserted streets. A foggy silence enveloped the atmosphere of the little community inside the walls. But Jerusalem's Jews did not yield easily. *Shuls* and *batey midrash* were packed just as they were on more sympathetic nights, and the sound of Torah defied the elements.

Reb Zimmel, the *shamash* of the Chevra Kadisha, made his way through the darkened alleys, trying to gather together a *minyan* of Jews to pay a deceased man his last respects. Reb Zeidel the silversmith had just passed away in his tiny room near the Nissan Bock Shul. A simple, unassuming person, Reb Zeidel had not left behind any family or relatives. Jerusalem custom did not permit a body to stay overnight without burial, and so Reb Zimmel was trying to get ten men from the Chevra Kadisha to perform the last rites and bring the body to proper burial.

Within half an hour, despite the fierce, raging storm, a dozen Chevra Kadisha members stood in the small room. The *tahara* was performed and the funeral procession marched toward Har haZeithim, ten men carrying the bier on their shoulders, their feet sinking into the blanket of snow and dirt. At they walked, the snow fell and covered them together with the bier, but they trudged on obliviously.

In the middle of the way, Reb Zimmel was suddenly overcome with weakness and could not continue further. His companions strongly urged him to return home and not endanger his health. He agreed reluctantly, and let himself be accompanied back by another member of the Chevra Kadisha who did not want the sick man to brave the elements alone on such a darkened night. Meanwhile the rest plodded forward, reached the foot of the mountain, and bravely struggled until the top. At this point they reminded themselves that they had forgotten to get instructions from Reb Zimmel regarding where the deceased was to be buried, for he had already purchased a plot in his lifetime. It was dark, late, and bitter cold. The poor men shivered in the relentless snow and wind which attacked their faces. There was a variance of opinion as to what to do with the body, but no one wanted the responsibility of deciding.

Finally the youngest of the group offered to go to Reb Zimmel's home, and find out from him exactly what to do. But the other members of the party refused to let him risk such a trip alone, to and back, through the raging elements. They were right, too, for they knew that he suffered from a weak constitution, living as he did in dire poverty, and spending all his days and nights in Torah study.

The oldest of the party now spoke up, "I suggest we bury Reb Zeidel in the nearest open grave. It is surely decreed by heaven that he be buried elsewhere than in the grave he chose for himself. Isn't Reb Zimmel's illness sufficient proof?" Reb Dan Trevish, who was experienced in these matters, continued, "We will request forgiveness from the *niftar*, and then proceed to bury him wherever we find a spot, on condition that when we do learn where the designated plot is, we will adjust the matter."

235

The Old City covered with snow

Everyone agreed and the deed was done. Reb Zeidel was laid to rest in a nearby open grave. It was then covered according to custom and a small stone, dyed in ink, marked the grave where lay "Reb Zeidel ben ——, may he rest in peace."

In the morning the Chevra Kadish men were surprised to discover that the simple smith had been buried near the grave of so holy a *tzaddik* that the greatest of Torah personalities did not dare dream of such an honor. And here an unknown smith, a lowly tradesman, occupied that highly coveted place!

Rav Yona Ba'al haNefesh

A KABBALIST AND *nistar,* whose very name aroused emotions of awe and fear, Rav Yona Ba'al haNefesh had been a close friend and confidant of the previous Rav of Jerusalem, Rav Yeshaya Bardaki, from his youth on. The Rav had treated his friend more like a teacher, bringing his problems to him, and studying Kabbala with him. Many stories were whispered about this Rav Yona Ba'al haNefesh, stories that concerned revelations from Eliyahu haNavi, wondrous tales about *tefilloth* that had been answered immediately, and so forth.

The place near Rav Yona's plot had purposely been kept empty for years. The members of the Chevra Kadisha had watched over it with hawk eyes, keeping it in readiness for the right person. Now that they had filled it so indiscriminately, they feared for the honor of the saintly Rav Yona.

Should they confess their mistake to Rav Shmuel Salant? He would surely grieve over the terrible error; he would be incensed as well. Were they to hide it from him? Was it at all possible to hide it?

There was no one who knew better than Rav Shmuel the true quality of Rav Yona Ba'al haNefesh, the pure ascetic who had spent his days in the Menachem Tziyon *beith midrash* of the Churva Shul in his *tallith* and *tefillin,* wrapped up in the holy secrets of Torah.

The members of the Chevra Kadisha remembered the

reason that Rav Shmuel had once given for the unusual epithet "Ba'al haNefesh." Rav Yona knew the *Nefesh haChayim* of Rav Chayim of Volozhin by heart, word for word. Having studied under that giant in his youth, Rav Yona could discourse volumes of *mussar* on every letter and letter-crown in that holy work.

Weary and worried, the members of the Chevra Kadisha shied away from the responsibility of a decision in such a weighty matter. They decided instead to call a general meeting of all the members and pose the problem to them.

It was a secret meeting, due to the nature of the problem. It was also a stormy assembly, especially since the older members vividly remembered the awe-inspiring visage of the saintly kabbalist, next to whom great Torah scholars dreamed of being buried yet trembled at the very idea! And now — woe to them if they confessed their sin; woe if they did not!

Reb Dan Trevish, the oldest member, interrupted the meeting with words that seemed to burst out of his mouth. "You must listen to me, my worthy associates, before we proceed to discuss the matter further. I must tell you an incident concerning Rav Yona Ba'al haNefesh which sticks in my mind and leaves me no peace.

"One day, in the year 5597," he began in a tear-choked voice, "Rav Yona suddenly appeared at the home of his friend, Rav Yeshaya Bardaki, attired in his *tallith* and *tefillin,* as was his custom. As the Rav was not home then, he left a note by the door:

> My dear friend, Rav Yeshaya, may your light shine,
> Since the purchase of the large synagogue for the Ashkenazim, the money for which has been donated by the philanthropist Reb Akiva Lehren, must soon be concluded, kindly inform your father-in-law, Rav

239

Yisrael, to come as soon as possible to Jerusalem to take care of the matter.

With Torah greetings,

Yona

"When Rav Yeshaya found the note in the doorway, he immediately sent a message to Safed, to his father-in-law, Rav Yisrael of Shklov, informing him of Rav Yona's advice that he come from Safed to Jerusalem.

"Rav Yisrael, who had heard much about Rav Yona, hurried to fulfill that *tzaddik's* request and left immediately for Jerusalem. On the following day he learned, together with all of Jewry, of the terrible earthquake that had seized Safed and the entire Galilee in which everything had been destroyed completely — homes with their inhabitants, *shuls*, *batey midrash*, even *tzaddikim*, were buried alive. Rav Yisrael was saved, however, because he had come to Jerusalem at Rav Yona's request."

That was the end of his tale. But even if he had wanted to comment or add some postscript, he wouldn't have been able to, for Reb Dan Trevish had fainted. He was overcome by the sheer greatness of the *tzaddik* next to whom he had buried the simple tradesman!

Reb Dan was duly aroused from his faint, but all the members were overcome with mixed emotions. Here and there someone fished out some forgotten memories of Rav Yona; one followed the other until the meeting resembled a fresh *hesped* — albeit so many years after his death.

It was getting late. The chairman called the meeting to order, reminding everyone that there still was a decision to be reached. But the breach between divergent opinions widened and the discussion raged on. One man suggested that all the members of the Chevra Kadisha go and prostrate themselves upon Rav Yona's grave, begging his forgiveness for the slight to his honor. Another demanded that Rav Shmuel Salant be informed at once, and that he alone should rule on what to do.

A thin partition separated the office of the Chevra Kadisha and the apartment of Rav Moshe Leib from Kutna, author of *Zayith Ra'anan*. As the noise and commotion increased, Rav Moshe sent his *shamash* to find out the cause of the noise. Immediately upon the *shamash's* entrance, all the men unanimously agreed to first ask Rav Moshe Leib for his advice. They all filed into Rav Moshe Leib's house.

Rav Moshe Leib was in excellent spirits just them. He was on the verge of completing his commentary on Mishnayoth, the *Tif'ereth Yerushalayim*, in which he had labored to answer all the difficulties that cropped up in Rabbi Akiva Eiger's glosses. Just a short while before, he had unraveled a challenging problem and had fallen asleep in exhaustion from the effort. In his sleep, Rabbi Akiva Eiger himself had appeared to him and disproved his answer. At this, Rav Moshe Leib had awakened in a joyous frame of mind, "Because that dream indicated that all my other answers are correct and acceptable to Rabbi Akiva Eiger."

The great scholar sat at the table leaning on his work. He listened to the collectively-told story and then replied good-humoredly, "My worthy friends, people dedicated to doing good: Leave this entire matter as it is. Let Rav Yona lie in peace; let Reb Zeidel lie in peace as well. If the heavenly court has no objection to their proximity, why should we object?"

In view of his greatness, all the members unanimously agreed to accept the Kutna *tzaddik's* decision. It was an honorable way out, and it relieved everyone of a heavy burden of guilt and responsibility. They all marveled at the simplicity of the logic. If the heavenly court did not object, then truly why should they make such a fuss? Their chosen authority, Rav Moshe Leib, surely knew of Rav Yona's greatness, yet thought it not to be of moment in view of the status quo.

The great man's decision was the last word. Everyone sensed it. The group dissolved, each going his way, and the matter was closed.

The Chevra Kadisha scribe entered the incident in the official record book. Next to Rav Yona's entry, which had been written many years before, he added the following postscript on a separate sheet:

> On the eve following the tenth of Teiveith, a simple tradesman named Reb Zeidel the smith passed away late at night. A heavy snow fell that night, covering all signs and directions to his grave. The frost was terrible; street-lights were extinguished, and the leader of the *chevra* became ill and could not participate in the burial. Through error and ignorance, Reb Zeidel was buried near the grave of Rav Yona Ba'al haNefesh, the great kabbalist, may he rest in peace. "May He forgive our sins and not destroy..."

The book was replaced in its cupboard, and the matter was forgotten. Thirty years passed and all the elders of that generation left the world. No one remained to remember the incident.

Reb Alter Shteper's Find

WHATEVER HAPPENED TO Reb Zeidel's little room after his death?

The room belonged to Kolel Suvalk. When the trustees of the kolel could not find a tenant willing to inhabit the cellar room which had only one tiny window, they rented it out to Reb Alter Shteper as a storage place for his workshop. In the year 5673, a fire broke out in the cellar, consuming all the lumber and furniture stored there by Reb Alter. The cellar was completely destroyed.

When the fire had been extinguished, Reb Alter entered the ruins to see if anything could still be salvaged. His account books had been there, among other things. Rummaging around among the debris, in the cracks and holes, he felt some scraps of paper. Thrusting his hand further, he was able to grasp a thick book written in ancient script, filled to bursting with tiny letters following one another without a breather for margins. The manuscript itself was singed and charred.

Reb Alter tried to read parts of it, but could make no headway. One thing was evident; it was a holy book containing Torah thoughts, and he must bring this ancient book to some recognized Torah authority for his opinion.

Times were hard. It was during World War One. Famine was claiming lives by the hordes. But though Jerusalem suffered, it did not relinquish its devotion to Torah study. The Yeshivoth were, as ever, brimful with scholars, young and old alike, all breathing and living their precious Torah, for they had nothing else.

Reb Alter Shteper walked into Torath Chayim yeshiva and laid his charred find upon the table. One scholar took the volume in his hands and looked through it briefly. He could see at once that it dealt with kabbalistic secrets, but it was hardly legible. Age and fire had wrought havoc upon the volume and the pages could not withstand the gentlest handling. The student rushed the manuscript to Rav Yitzchak Yerucham Diskin. He too, could barely make out the words. Suddenly he saw an inscription that made tears rush to his eyes. The last page was signed, "Zeidel the Smith."

Apparently the *gaon* of Kutna had known about him all along...

The Sugar Bird

"YANKELE! YANKELE!" came the combined cry of a hoarse male and a shrill-voiced female. The neighbors were not alarmed. They knew that Reb Zalman and his wife Chana were once again summoning their six-year-old son home.

As for Yankele, he was busy playing in the large square across the Rechov haYehudim, but his parents' cry succeeded in reaching him. Yankele's skinny feet stood with some difficulty in a pair of worn, misshapen shoes, and his legs were covered by trousers whose patches had already worn out. His emaciated shoulders bore a faded, shabby shirt over which was lopsidedly flung an *arba kanfoth* whose fringes straggled limply down. His head was bedecked with a white yarmulka and framed by a pair of black curly sidelocks. His forehead, lined and pale, sat above a pair of black, burning eyes. That was Yankele.

Yankele was the happiest creature on earth at the time his parents' cries reached his ears. He was busy licking a red bird-shaped lollypop, this treasure being the reason he had sought refuge — to dedicate all his senses to enjoying and savoring that sucker.

There he stood blissfully, thrusting the sweet into his mouth, sucking hard to get its full flavor and then removing it. Each lick was an individual act. Between each act he would raise the lollypop to his eyes, testing it to see how much it had diminished since the last lick, and calculating how much longer it could possibly be before he remained with an empty stick in his hand.

When his parents' call reached his ears, he was not caught by surprise. In fact, he had come this distance expressly in order to avoid and evade it. His first reaction was to suck quickly, even chew his treasure, quickly swallow his sweet spittle, and throw away the stick as if nothing had happened. Then he changed his mind. No, he had waited for such a treat far too long to relinquish it so quickly. How often had he seen his friends sucking such a sweet and felt his bones quaking with desire!

One lick and another lick, and his parents themselves appeared. Yankele barely managed to thrust the sugar bird into his pants pocket before his father's thundering voice demanded, "What are you doing here? Didn't you hear us calling you, Yankele?"

"N-no, n-no, I didn't hear," poor Yankele stammered, swallowing his sugary saliva. "The wind blew my *yarmulka* into the square and I w-went to pick it up."

Yankele's mother had meanwhile grabbed his hand and was dragging him homeward after her, protesting to her husband, "Zalman, don't make such a commotion on the street."

The Golden Lira

THE MINIATURE PROCESSION marched homeward, first
Chana dragging her one and only son, Yankele, and after
these two stalked Reb Zalman murmuring half aloud,
"The very last pound. Oh dear me, all I did was leave my
drawer open and now the pound is gone! "

When he reached home Reb Zalman ran once again to
the drawer that was always locked. Its contents were
spilled all over the table: a few tins of tobacco, some
empty and some full, several packets of cigarette paper of
his own making, three ancient and worn-out receipt books
which dated to the better days when he had owned a
flour mill and had been a man of independent means, his
wife's *kethuva,* and some tuition receipts from Yankele's
rebbi.

Everything on the table was present and accounted for.
All, that is, except for the golden lira coin, the last remaining relic of the good times that had once been. Reb Zalman, who had been silent until now, asked his son angrily,
"Yankele, are you the one who removed the gold lira?"

Then it was Chana's turn. "Yankele my dear, tell us the
truth. Don't you see how unhappy your parents are now
that the last penny has disappeared? We will have nothing
to eat! Just tell the truth and I will buy you a sugar bird."
The tears rolled down her cheeks and on to the boy's
own face.

"What are you begging him for?" Zalman's voice

247

thundered again. "It's a foregone conclusion that he is the thief. He probably took it while you were looking over the *burghil*. [This was actually chicken feed, but Yerushalmim ate it out of desperation in times of hunger.] I went to light a cigarette outside in the sun with a magnifying glass. Actually I noticed him sneaking out of the house and then running but it never occurred to me... And when I went back in, the coin was gone! Oy! Oy!" he groaned. "I wanted a cigarette. I craved a cigarette and this is my reward!"

His anger grew from minute to minute. "I'll break his bones," he shouted and raised a fist over the thin, emaciated boy. Had it not been for Chana who rushed to her son's aid, the boy would have remembered that blow for many days.

Zalman thrust his hand into the boy's pocket. It came out all sticky, grasping the lollypop. Yankele burst into tears at the sight of his precious sugar bird, already half gone, being placed on the table. A feeling of remorse flooded his little body as he slowly began to realize the value of the coin he had taken. It began to dawn on him that his act would force his parents to beg for bread. He recalled the words his *rebbi* had taught in *cheider* — where he happened to be one of the best students — concerning Rachel's taking her father's idols. The *rebbi* had stressed the severity of the punishment for stealing, even though in this case Rachel's intentions had been the purest. Yankele remembered and Yankele trembled. He now began to beg his parents' forgiveness.

The little boy's tears somewhat softened his father's harsh aspect. He asked Yankele where he had gotten the sugar bird from and Yankele confessed in a tear-choked voice that he had taken the coin from the drawer and bought the sweet from Rachamim the sweets peddler.

"You gave the whole lira for the sugar bird?"

"Come, let's go find that Rachamim the peddler," said another tear-choked voice from the outdoor kitchen.

At the Peddler's

ONCE AGAIN THE THREE proceeded outside with purposeful strides. First marched Reb Zalman, then his wife Chana towing a weeping Yankele along. Their hurried steps and the unusual spectacle of Reb Zalman bearing a half-licked lollypop aroused the curiosity of the neighborhood. As they marched forward they accumulated a train of curious spectators who followed behind, some who had managed to hear part of the story, some who just smelled something interesting in the air.

Rachamim's little shop was on a street corner. There he sat on a small platform in his barefooted glory, wearing his usual wide pantaloons and loose shirt, his head covered by a faded red turban. His wares were displayed on the counter in front of him: yellow, green, and red sugar birds whose sticks were thrust into a cactus plant. These were his only wares, but he displayed them proudly for they were the products of his making.

In a trilingual singsong chant, Rachamim advertised his wares to Arab customers, Hebrew-speaking customers, and Yiddish-speaking customers. He was surrounded by potential customers, thin children who ate up his sugar birds with their hungry eyes. Among them were the fortunate ones who were able to acquire such a prize and, being the goodhearted Yerushalmi children that they were, to share their fortune with friends and playmates.

Reb Zalman contained his anger as he approached the stand. "Did my boy buy a sugar bird from you?" he asked.

"Yes," answered Rachamim, fingering the red beads which were his surety against the evil eye. He recognized Yankele from better times — a year and a half ago — when the boy had been one of his good customers.

"How much did he pay you?"

"What do you mean, how much? Ten prutot. Don't you know, Reb Zalman, that I have been selling my goods for the same price for these past few years despite the hard times?" Rachamim began once again to elaborate on the merits of his goods in his familiar chant.

"He didn't give you a golden lira?" Reb Zalman interrupted the chant heatedly.

"A golden *lira*? A *golden* lira? I never in all my days held a golden lira in my hand!"

As Reb Zalman began to raise his voice, his wife Chana felt it necessary to intervene. "Rachamim, you are a Jew. Have some pity. It was our very last lira." Her words were hardly discernible because of her tears.

As soon as Rachamim felt the matter to be serious he emptied out all the six pockets sewn into his pantaloons. Out came ten-pruta pieces and more ten-pruta pieces. "See," he exclaimed vehemently, "I didn't even earn enough today to buy myself a *burghil* pita!"

The conversation, which grew more heated with each passing moment, aroused the attention of the whole street. Soon a ring of storekeepers surrounded the central figures. When they learned that a golden lira was the question in point, they remained transfixed in their places. All traffic stopped. Even the water-carrier with his four large cans of precious liquid could barely pass by. His cargo dripped enough valuable drops to quench the thirst of a little Jerusalem boy before he could squeeze through.

251

There was a conflict of opinions. The majority believed Reb Zalman. He was known as an important person, an honest merchant who knew Torah too. His only boy, Yankele, also had the reputation of being one of the best students in the *cheider,* for whom a golden future was predicted. Surely if Yankele said that he gave the coin to Rachamim and Reb Zalman vouched that the coin had been a golden lira, surely they were telling the truth!

But a strong minority also felt the need to praise Rachamim's own renowned honesty. "How can one know?" they argued. "A boy is a boy and you can't rely on what he says."

The discussion continued for a long time, Reb Zalman burning with anger. He threatened Rachamim loudly, his wife supporting him with gentler tones of beseeching, and Rachamim, not one to be bested, invited anyone to "search all my things. If you find that lira in my possession you may hang me." This invitation was supported by the graphic gesture of finger across throat.

The litigants and the audience soon tired of the affair. When the noise subsided somewhat, the voice of an important-looking Jew was heard, "Yidden, why must you ruin your health in anger and shouting? Your health is more precious that gold. Go to the *beith din* and set a date for a *din-*Torah. The *dayanim* of Jerusalem should surely be able to throw some light on the matter."

Reb Zalman needed no more than a hint. He was already running toward the rooms in the courtyard of the Churva Shule where the Jerusalem *beith din* sat.

The Din-Torah

THE DIN-TORAH WAS SET for two days hence, and Reb
Zalman returned hurriedly to inform Rachamim the
peddler. Reb Zalman and his wife were once again seen
marching down the Street of the Jews, Reb Zalman com-
plaining aloud, "What shall we do now? It's been half a
year since the flour mill stopped doing business and I
haven't earned a penny throughout this famine." He did
not forget to add a short prayer to his Father in Heaven.
"See my misery," he begged. "Forgive my sins and please
make the peddler have a change of heart and return the
stolen money."

Chana, no less broken by the loss, was somehow able
to gather her strength and console her husband. "Look
at the multitude of Jews walking the streets who never
had a golden lira in their drawers. And they are not dying
of hunger."

When they returned home Reb Zalman tried looking
into his pockets once more. Who knows, he might yet find
some coins. But all he found was the half-eaten sugar bird
he had confiscated from his son. Nothing more. He laid
the lollypop on the table once again, took out a small
Tehilim, and sat in a corner silently mouthing chapter
after chapter.

Yankele had meanwhile returned from his afternoon
session in *cheider*. He *davvened ma'ariv*, recited the Shma-
before-retiring and laid himself down to sleep. He had no

253

need to *bench,* for he had not eaten a morsel; the house was completely bare.

Two days passed, and the eagerly expected day of judgment arrived. Both parties appeared much before the appointed time. Rachamim the peddler was dressed in holiday garb out of respect for the *dayanim.* Gone were his baggy pants of many pockets and his bare feet. Instead he wore trousers and sandals bought from an Arab especially for the occasion. The time came, and the two men entered the courtroom. Reb Zalman began by relating all the particulars of the incident. Rachamim, not in the least intimidated, kept on insisting that all he had received from the boy was a ten-pruta piece. Rav Nachum Wallenstein, the chief *dayan,* summoned Yankele from the Etz Chayim *cheider* which — like most Jerusalem institutions — adjoined the Churva courtyard.

Yankele appeared in a fright, heightened by the *dayan*'s awe-inspiring face, but the Rav stroked the youthful cheek with his velvety hand and the boy calmed down.

"Did you learn in *chumash,* my dear boy, that it is forbidden to lie?"

Yankele happily nodded in the affirmative. The Rav now took out two coins, a golden lira and a ten-pruta bronze piece. He then asked Yankele to point to the coin that he had taken from his father's drawer.

Without hesitating, the boy pointed to the gold piece.

"And what did you do with the coin?"

"I bought a sugar bird from Rachamim."

Yankele's interrogation was over. He was sent back to *cheider.*

The head of the *beith din* now turned to the peddler. "Rachamim," he said sternly, "are you prepared to swear that such a gold lira did not come into your hand?" The rabbi meanwhile motioned to the *shamash* to prepare the necessary accessories for swearing.

"I c-cannot swear," Rachamim stuttered in confusion.

"If you are telling the truth, why can't you swear?" the *dayan* asked suspiciously.

"My father, may he rest in Gan Eden — Your Honor surely knew him — taught us to be careful not to swear even for the truth. He would always repeat the words of our Sages upon the verse, 'Fear your God and worship Him, and cling to Him, and swear in His Name,' saying, 'If you immerse yourself in Torah and its commandments and you cling to Him, then you are permitted to swear in His name. If not, then you may not swear.' I saw him in a dream just last night and I remembered his words. I therefore refuse to swear."

"If you refuse to swear, are you then prepared to pay the lira?"

"To pay? From what should I pay?"

The chief *dayan* leaned toward his fellow *dayanim* who sat beside him and they consulted briefly. Then he turned to the peddler once more, "If you do not swear that you did not receive the golden lira, then you are compelled to pay. But we will allow you to pay the money in installments."

Rachamim accepted the decision with equanimity.

The story of the golden lira and the *pesak din* became the topic of the day in the destitute Jerusalem of that era. Between *mincha* and *ma'ariv,* when all news was exchanged, the episode was tossed around verbally. Now everyone agreed that Rachamim must have received the lira. Otherwise he would not have refused to take an oath. Swearing to the truth was far simpler than burdening oneself with unnecessary debts in those difficult times.

But even with public consensus in favor of Reb Zalman,

255

someone did stand up in the peddler's defense. "Even so, one cannot evaluate the soul of a simple Jew. If he is indeed a liar, why should he hesitate to swear to a lie?" But this lone opinion was shouted down, "Nonsense. Is Rachamim such a *tzaddik* as to undertake such a staggering debt if he is innocent, and then refuse to swear into the bargain?"

The Truth Is Revealed

Several years passed, and the war became a thing of the past. Now the English ruled instead of the Turks. Trade relations with the world were resumed and Jerusalem forgot its famine. Reb Zalman was able to reopen his flour mill and resume his former station in life. And now that he had the means, Reb Zalman returned to his Torah studies and to his communal activities. Yankele continued to excel in *cheider,* and his parents reaped Jewish *nachass* from him.

The days of plenty banished the memory of the lean years together with most of the chapter of Rachamim and the golden lira; a debt of only a few prutoth remained.

One wintry, rainy evening, while Reb Zalman sat studying in his *gemara* by the stove that diffused a warm, pleasant atmosphere in the room, and Chana plied her needlework busily, someone knocked at the door. The couple looked at one another in surprise. Who would come knocking at such a late hour on such a stormy night.

The door opened hesitantly, and Moshe Chayim, the reputedly unlucky blacksmith, entered. He wanted to speak to Reb Zalman. "Alone," he begged. Obviously, the matter was pressing because he refused to sit down. Chana understood that her presence was unwanted and left the room, closing the door behind her.

"You surely recall, Reb Zalman, what happened to you

with the golden lira during the war years and the ensuing *din*-Torah with Rachamim the peddler."

Reb Zalman remembered the episode like a nightmare. It was not at all pleasant to recall the degradation he had suffered for the sake of some *burghil* bread.

Moshe Chayim the blacksmith continued, "It is that episode that has brought me here. I have come to confess the truth, which has been weighing on me like a heavy rock. The lira that your son removed from the drawer did not reach the hands of Rachamim. It reached mine..."

Although Reb Zalman found this subject and the painful memories it aroused distasteful, he now looked at his neighbor in wide-eyed surprise and curiosity. The blacksmith hung his head in shame but felt compelled to get the whole truth out now that he had started. "On that day I went outside to seek a small loan. For two days my children had not tasted a morsel of food, and they were bloated with hunger. I didn't find any likely source, for I had already borrowed all the money I could after having sold all my personal goods. About to return home with my disappointing results, my knees buckled under me and I leaned against a railing on Rechov haYehudim trying not to collapse altogether under the strain of three days' fasting.

"Suddenly I noticed your Yankele running to the candy vendor with a golden lira in his hand. I went over to him and stroked his cheek while exchanging my last bronze ten-pruta coin — which couldn't even buy a flask of water — for his golden lira. He didn't notice the exchange, and went on straight to the sweets peddler. As soon as Yankele had disappeared from view, my conscience began hurting me. I considered returning the tainted money and even began walking in the direction of your house. But on the way I said to myself, "Moshe Chayim, your children at home are bloated from famine while other children have golden liras floating around in their homes! In these days when Jews roam the streets vainly searching for some edible peels from between Arab feet to sustain the lives of their children, a little boy goes and buys himself a sugar bird! And with a golden lira, no less! Under such circumstances you may surely allow yourself, Moshe Chayim, to borrow the lira and later, when God eases your situation, you can repay it.'

"I was weak enough to talk myself into keeping the money. Unable to withstand the temptation, I rushed to the market to buy some lentils and a few coals. My children's eyes lit up; their dry bones warmed a bit from the soup. Later, when I went outside and heard the noise that the lost lira had aroused, I again had feelings of remorse, but it was already too late. I did not have the moral fiber to go and confess that I had taken the money and thereby besmirch my name and family."

Moshe Chayim continued his tale with tears in his eyes. "It's difficult to describe what I went through during that period. My sin smote my conscience and disturbed my peace day and night. If everyone waited eagerly for the war to end, I looked forward to it doubly. I could not wait for the day when I would be able to return the stolen lira. As soon as the war was over, I did indeed begin to save penny by penny until I had laid away the entire gold lira. Now I am able to pay it all back."

He breathed heavily, took out two gold coins from his pocket and laid them on the table. "A thief pays double — one lira for you and one for Rachamim the righteous. I robbed you both; I robbed you both of your peace and brought you both to shame.

"Please forgive me, Reb Zalman, and be my messenger to Rachamim the vendor. Ask his forgiveness in my name. I am certain that I could not bear to see his face and to

259

stand in the four cubits of such an exalted *tzaddik* who refused to swear for the truth, preferring rather to place himself in a position of mockery and shame and pay a debt he had not incurred despite his own poverty.

"Forgive me, Reb Zalman," he repeated and fell down in a faint.

Reb Zalman stood transfixed, unable to gather his thoughts together. He did not even have enough presence of mind to do something for the prostrate figure that lay before him. But Chana, who had heard the resounding thud, came rushing to see what had happened. As she opened the door, Reb Zalman managed to cry out, "Water! Water!" Before she could act, the blacksmith had gotten to his feet and was beating a hasty retreat out the front door with an embarrassed "Good night" on his lips.

Chana's curiosity was aroused by the strange proceedings, all the more so when her eyes lit on the two gold liras that gleamed on the table.

"What happened here, Zalman?" she asked.

Rez Zalman shook himself back to reality like one who had just been aroused from a deep sleep.

"Oh, Chana! How true is the saying that one cannot begin to value the soul of a Jew!"

The candy vendor's soul was even more difficult to value than Reb Zalman and the rest of Jerusalem Jews suspected. The only people, in fact, who could appreciate the true worth of the wide-pantalooned peddler were his friends in the Beith-El yeshiva of kabbalists and *nistarim*, for they saw him come there for fifteen years straight, night after night, while the rest of Jerusalem slept soundly. Reb Shalom Gibbor, the porter, and the other *nistarim*, knew his true value full well, for they spent three hours together each night immersed in the works of the greatest of kabbalists, the Ari of blessed memory. They came silently and went silently so that no one ever knew of their holy ways.

When the Jews of Jerusalem got an inkling of who Rachamim really was, when they learned something of his holy ways, they inadvertently robbed him of his private treasure. Rachamim found no more joy in life. And one short week after he got back the golden lira his presence was requested in the heavenly realms.

Reb Shalom the Mighty

THE JEWS' STREET was the main artery of the lifestream in the Old City. Long and narrow, full to overflowing, the street boasted store upon tiny store, leaning against each other and elbowing for precious space along both sides. Flour sacks, sugar sacks, rice sacks, and wheat sacks vied for breathing room with oil barrels and herring barrels, all crowding upon one another in such profusion that one couldn't tell what belonged to whom.

Noise and confusion abounded from morning to night. Voices of shopkeepers, customers, and porters from various Jewish sects mingled with the clamor of gentile villagers, policemen, and Moslem effendi to compose a weird symphony. A single purpose united them all: that of providing for their families and of making some margin of profit through buying or selling in the market.

In the midst of such tumult who would take note of a new Jewish face trying to push its way into the sea of humanity already there? Dozens of strange and new types wandered around on Jews' Street. Each dawning day brought its fresh face, be it Polish, Russian, Hungarian, Yemeni, Persian, or Sefaradi, seeking as always to strike roots somewhere along the street and join the multitude of single-purposed men striving to provide for their families. Some were beggars; others sought gainful employment through any kind of labor. Even the porting line had a profusion of eager hands grabbing for each sack and barrel to be transported from place to place.

One new face did, however, manage to catch people's attention in the middle of all this anonymity, almost as soon as it appeared on the scene. Like a walking tree, the new figure strode down the main street, a full head taller than other men. The stranger wore a black, faded capote held together with a thick rope, a pair of heavy boots, and a crushed hat. One could not see much of his face, covered as it was with a hairy black and white beard that flowed luxuriously down his chest.

He really most resembled a giant who had stepped out of a fairy tale, an ogre sowing fear and panic wherever he trod — until one looked up into his eyes. Then one was captivated by a pair of warm, smiling, gentle, dark eyes like the eyes of a young boy.

And this boy-giant sought a livelihood. Approaching one of the bountiful-looking shops that bulged with sacks and barrels, he asked the storekeeper, "Reb Yid, could you use a porter?" The deep but gentle bass voice commanded the busy shopkeeper's attention. He intended at first to send him off with the usual negative reply, but when the shopkeeper looked into the eyes of the friendly giant standing in his doorway, his heart leaped into his throat. How could he send the stranger away? He was new and surely needed a source of nourishment for his gigantic frame.

"Yes, I need one. What's your name?"

"Shalom," came the reply from the man, who had already taken the sack from the shopkeeper's hand into his giant one.

"All right, then, Reb Shalom. I have use for you. Come in, please, and arrange these sacks of sugar and rice that arrived just today into a pile there in the corner."

"Surely," replied the friendly giant with alacrity. "Right away!"

Reb Shalom began hauling the heavy sacks. But hauling was a word that described the activities of the puffing porters who had brought them. In Reb Shalom's huge arms they were like playthings. In the wink of an eye he had them in the corner and piled one above the other as neat as could be. The storekeeper stood back and gaped as Reb Shalom came and waited patiently, humbly, for his fee.

The storekeeper did not know what to say. He dropped a decent coin into the waiting palm and finally found his tongue. "You did a very nice job of it, Reb Shalom. Pass by tomorrow and I will find some more work for you."

"Thank you," replied Reb Shalom simply. "I will come, please God."

The news spread rapidly. Reb Shalom's prowess earned him the nickname of 'the Gibbor' on his very first day. That evening when the shopkeepers of the main street gathered to *davven mincha* and *ma'ariv* in the *shtiblach* of the Churva Shul, they had only one subject on their lips.

"Who is he?"

"Where is he from?"

"Surely he is a *nistar*."

"He's probably some Russian landowner who converted."

"He's one of the thirty-six secret *tzaddikim*."

"No, he's only a plain ignoramus."

"We'll live and see."

At this very moment Reb Shalom himself was seated at one of the long tables in the *shtiblach* listening to a *shi'ur* in Ein Yaakov.

From the very start, Reb Shalom was the porter in greatest demand along the entire street. Not only did his strength stand him in good stead but his obedience as well. His livelihood was assured. Each morning before sunrise Reb Shalom would set forth from his little room bordering on the Arab quarter where he lived in solitude, and head to the Churva Shul for a *vathikin minyan*. Each evening he would return for *mincha* and a *shi'ur* in Ein Yaakov. After the market was empty he would return home with a loaf of black bread under one arm and a few greens tied up in his red handkerchief in his other hand.

The room Reb Shalom inhabited was in a deserted, half-ruined courtyard. His next-door neighbors were Arabs with whom he never had any contact. They would occca- sionally peek into his windows to see what the strange Jew was up to.

A Russian? they would wonder. *Did he hide money sacks under the floor tiles?* they asked themselves.

The Tehilim Society

SEVERAL WEEKS PASSED from Reb Shalom's first appearance. During this interval no one learned any new information about the giant porter with the eyes of a child, surely not from Reb Shalom himself, who hardly ever spoke.

One Friday afternoon after his *mikveh*-bath, Reb Shalom stopped by the Chavilya sweet shop. He pointed out the wares he desired and, after they were weighed for him, he paid and took his packages home.

Reb Shalom had noticed that on Shabbath between *mincha* and *ma'ariv* all the little boys of Rechov ha-Yehudim would gather in the Churva courtyard and run wild. Their good-natured shouts and fights would disturb all the adults learning there. Reb Shalom planned to gather them together into one of the *shtiblach*, sit them down around the table, and distribute his goodies while they said a few chapters of *Tehilim* until it was time for *ma'ariv*.

He arrived at *mincha* that Shabbath with his pockets stuffed. After *mincha* he called one of the boys to him, and said, "My pockets are filled with sweets. Tell your friends around outside to come into one of the *shtiblach* and they will get some."

His soft, gentle eyes and kind voice won him their confidence. Within minutes Reb Shalom had twenty little boys seated at a table inside, he at its head. "Children, if you come here every Shabbath you will get some sweets. But first let us say some *Tehilim*."

The little boys responded like cherubs warming to a benevolent uncle. Reb Shalom took some *Tehilim* volumes off a shelf and distributed them among the children. He took one for himself and began singing, *"Ashrey themimay darech."* He was echoed by twenty childish voices repeating verse for verse.

The Churva courtyard rang out with the praises of David the son of Yishai. The wonderful bass voice of their leader harmonized with the trebles of his lively little choir. The Churva filled with people who came to hear this symphony of heart-rending poignancy.

Reb Shalom the Gibbor earned his world-to-come on that Shabbath. The simple, humble, and shy porter had established the very first Chevra Tehilim in Jerusalem, the first of the many that have since flourished and continue to this very day! The recital of *Tehilim* between *mincha* and *ma'ariv* became a custom — accompanied by the reward of cookies, candies, and sunflower seeds.

Reb Shalom Tries a New Trade

As a result of Reb Berel the Waker's death, Reb Shalom acquired a new vocation about two years after he came to Jerusalem. A good friend of Reb Shalom, the professional waker left a will requesting that his job — arousing Jerusalem's Jews at the break of dawn to their daily task of serving their Creator — be filled by Reb Shalom.

His route began in the Old City streets. From there he would exit through Jaffa Gate and continue his rounds through the neighborhoods of the new Jerusalem. Mei'a Sh'arim, Nachalath Shiv'a, and Yemin Moshe. When it was already light he would go to the Churva Shul and *davven*.

The Arab city watchmen knew him well, and would often accompany him along parts of his route, even helping him sing his song.

Neither cold nor heat prevented Reb Shalom from performing his morning duty. His greatest satisfaction came when the Jerusalem Jews began responding to his calls by streaming to the *shuls,* and he was able to hear the first sounds of Torah and prayer emerging from within. Then he would continue his rounds, waking the lazier inhabitants who had not risen at his first cries.

As Jerusalem Jewry rushed to serve the Creator with *tallith* and *tefillin* sacks under their arms, they looked upon their waker with awe. Relentlessly continuing his rounds, circling and ever returning to the central point of the synagogues to see if the benches were all occupied, Reb Shalom would not stop until he was satisfied that his task was completed for the day.

Jokesters used to say that his familiar figure was alluded to in the verse from the Torah, "And I shall bring peace (*shalom*) in the land and you shall lie down without disturbances." When Reb Shalom will rest in the ground — after 120 years — then you will be able to lie down without disturbance, for then he will no longer disturb Yerushalmim from their sleep.

Rav Chayim Sonnenfeld Saves a Soul

ONE MORNING, as Reb Shalom was making his usual rounds singing his daily refrain, he was ambushed by a *maskil*. His enemy was a Jew who had attended the banned secular schools in his youth and had forsaken all that was holy. As Reb Shalom approached on that particular morning, the man threw a vessel of dirty water into his face.

Reb Shalom did not tell a soul about this incident, accepting his shame in silence. The only people who knew of his degradation were the members of the man's family. He himself died a sudden death that very day, though no one connected the sad event with the shaming of Reb Shalom.

Two days after the event, Reb Shalom passed the same house upon his regular rounds. Suddenly a huge, frightful black dog bounded out and threw itself at his feet. Reb Shalom the Mighty, not one to be afraid of any creature, paid no attention to this beast even though it followed him throughout his rounds that day. *So what*, thought Reb Shalom to himself, *so what if a wild dog runs around after me.*

On the following day the incident repeated itself. Reb Shalom would not have paid any attention to the dog or the strange fact of its appearing from that particular house, had it not happened morning after morning for five days in a row. After he had completed his route on the fifth day, Reb Shalom went to the *beith din* in the Churva courtyard and feelingly revealed the strange story.

The *rabbanim* listened to the story in awe. They tried at first to wave the incident away as a coincidence or as a figment of the imagination. But Reb Shalom had been prepared for this possibility. He had planted two witnesses that morning by the house and the two men had seen exactly how the dog had run up to the waker and whined at his feet. Not only that, but the members of the family had been on the scene, forewarned by the witnesses. The family had laughed the incident away until someone had called the dog by the deceased man's name. Then the dog had suddenly gone berserk. He had cavorted wildly, jumped up, scratched at the windows of the house and behaved altogether strangely.

"The family," reported the witnesses, "is completely broken. They say they are ready to accept any penance, any program for repentance that the *beith din* prescribes."

The *rabbanim* were convinced that this was no fairy tale, that it was all really true. The matter was so serious and complex, they decided, that Rav Chayim Sonnenfeld, then Rav of the city, should be called in.

This was not the first time that Rav Chayim had been called upon to resolve a difficult case, but age and weakness had made such appearances rather rare lately. This case though was an exception, the *dayanim* felt, and he must be consulted. The *rosh beith din* himself, Rav Mordechai Leib Rubin, went to the Rav's house in Batey Machseh to beg him to come. Rav Chayim was not at home at the time. "He is at the Etz Chayim *cheider*," his wife said. "Oy," panted Rav Mordechai, exhausted from the effort, "he was nearby all the time and we didn't even know it!"

What is the Rav doing at such an hour at Etz Chayim?

271

The Rav Av Beth Din, Rav Mordechai Leib Rubin

*One of the first neighborhoods outside of the city walls —
Meya She'arim*

wondered Rav Mordechai as he hurried back. Along the way who should he meet but Rav Chayim himself. Unable to contain his curiosity, Rav Mordechai asked the Rav what he had been doing in the *cheider*.

"Nothing special," answered Rav Chayim. "One of my grandsons will enter the age of mitzvoth in a few days. I went to ask his *rebbi* to teach the boy the 613 mitzvoth. Generally, it is accepted that the boy says a *pilpul*, but I think that if he could recite all the mitzvoth on the day that they are incumbent on him, it would be the nicest *derasha* one could expect to hear."

Rav Mordechai told the Rav what had brought him to his home in such a rush. He added that the other *dayanim* were awaiting them both at the courtroom.

Rav Chayim agreed to accompany Rav Mordecai. He knew Reb Shalom well. The man ate at his table every Shabbath Mevarchim, as well as on Yamim Tovim. The Rav's grandchildren used to tell how Reb Shalom was always honored with the first recital of the Ma Nishtana on the Seider night. It seemed that Rav Chayim found unique pleasure in Reb Shalom's special pleasant melody.

The Rav required no confirmation of Reb Shalom's story. He trusted Reb Shalom explicitly and knew that if he said something it was no figment of imagination, but the solid truth.

Rav Chayim entered the courtroom. Everyone stood up until he was seated at the head of the table. Then he summoned the members of the deceased's family who stood and waited shamefaced while he consulted with the other *dayanim*. Rav Mordechai Leib, honored with announcing the judicial decision, arose and declaimed in thunderous tones.

"Your father sinned grievously. His sin is too terrible to bear. He wanted to silence the eternal voice of the Jew,

273

the authentic voice of Yisrael, which wakens Jerusalem Jewry to serve their Maker. His punishment was therefore to transmigrate to the form of a dog which disturbs his own family's peace while others sleep and gather strength for Torah study and worship.

"According to the Rav's suggestion and the agreement of the other members of the *beith din*, we hereby prescribe the following program of repentance:

"Jerusalem is full, thank God, of *batey midrash* that harbor Torah scholars who learn throughout the nights. Your father desired to still the voice of Torah, to uproot it. We therefore suggest that after begging Reb Shalom's forgiveness, you shall, from today on, supply these scholars with warm drink every single night. And on cold winter nights you shall supply firewood to keep them warm as well. You will thereby atone for your father's sin."

The sons accepted the penance upon themselves immediately. And true to their word, from that night on, the members of the dead man's family carried tea and coffee to the *shuls* and *batey midrash* in Jerusalem. Even to this very day, one of the man's grandsons continues to provide fuel to warm Jerusalem's places of study.

The *rosh beith din* turned to Reb Shalom with these instructions: "When you again meet this poor soul, tell it, in the name of the Rav of Jerusalem and the members of the *beith din*, that its sin has been atoned for and that you forgive it with complete heart." Reb Shalom nodded his head in agreement.

And on the following morning, as Reb Shalom came to the house of the accursed soul, the black dog once again jumped forward to greet him. Remembering his instructions, Reb Shalom announced: "In the name of the great Rav of Jerusalem, Rav Yosef Chayim Sonnenfeld, and in the name of the *beith din* of the Holy City, I hereby inform you that your sin has been absolved and I, too, forgive you with a full heart."

The dog immediately vanished and never appeared again.

That very day Reb Shalom went to the *beith din* to inform them of the incident, and to thank them for having redeemed the unfortunate soul of the person who had shamed him.

The Living Dead

REB SHALOM LIVED A LONG, full life. Almost two full generations of Yerushalmim knew him. As surely as he would have risked his life to protect his fellow-Jews in life, so did he take pains to provide for them after their death.

Ever since the founding of the old settlement in Jerusalem, the dead were removed from the city on stretchers made of two long wooden poles. And, as was the custom, no dead body was kept overnight inside the city walls. The members of the Chevra Kadisha, undeterred by the raging elements, faithfully buried the dead even on snowy, stormy nights. They would proceed through the Dung Gate and down the slope to the Mount of Olives.

When the gunsmoke of Zionist aspirations and pan-Arab nationalism began to becloud the skies of Eretz Yisrael, the members of the Chevra Kadisha found their work increasingly dangerous. Wild Arabs would attack funeral processions and throw stones, often causing the poor Chevra Kadisha members to drop their charge and run for their lives.

Such an unfortunate incident occurred during one of Baron Rothschild's stays in Jerusalem. The Baron happened to pass at the precise moment that an Arab band of ruffians was attacking the funeral procession of a lone man who had no people to mourn him. He stared aghast as the body was abandoned and the pallbearers ran for their lives. The Baron immediately went to the Arab authorities and made them promise to send a group of policemen to accompany every funeral that had few or no mourners.

But Rothschild's action did not solve the problem completely. It was Reb Shalom who came to the rescue with a daring plan. Approaching the head of the Chevra Kadisha, he proposed to pretend that he had died. "I'll dress myself in *tachrichim* and lie upon the stretcher. Then the Chevra Kadisha will remove me from the city through the Dung Gate. They will probably be attacked by Arabs. When they lay me down and run for refuge, I will do my part, with the help of God. I'll jump up and take care of them."

The members of the Chevra Kadisha were called to listen to the novel idea. At first they refused to hear of such outlandish tactics, but Reb Shalom the Gibbor lived up to his name and won them over to his scheme.

It all happened exactly as planned. As soon as the members of the Chevra Kadisha, bearing their mock corpse, stepped outside of the city walls through the small gate, they were attacked. They put down their load, stopped their recital of *Yosheiv Beseither* in the middle, and ran back inside the gate. Reb Shalom waited a few minutes and then arose in his snowy white shrouds and ran at the hoodlums. Besides frightening the living daylights out of them, he made mincemeat out of them. Here he broke an arm, there he smashed some teeth. One Arab managed to run away with only a black eye, another escaped with a bashed-in nose. All the Arabs ran helter-skelter calling on "Allah Akbar," the great God, to help them. But Reb Shalom did not let them escape until each one had some souvenir of the event on his body.

The superstitious Arabs were certain that the Jewish

corpse had come to life. That very day a group of effendi appeared at the Rav's home. They begged him to forgive their people, promising that from then on they would guarantee safe passage to all funeral parties. But they made the Rav promise in turn that he would pray on their behalf and insure them that God's wrath would not overtake them.

From that time on there were no more problems. Reb Shalom had prevailed.

Holy in Life and Holy in Death

AS TIME PASSED, Reb Shalom's Arab neighbors grew convinced that he had sacks of gold hidden under his floor tiles. How could they know that he distributed all his earnings to the beggars at the Kothel each day and that nothing remained after he had bought his meager provisions?

One Shabbath when Reb Shalom returned from the Kothel to get his candies for the *Tehilim* group, he found uninvited guests ransacking his room. His Arab neighbors fell upon him and beat him savagely. Reb Shalom fell on his bed in a faint. He lay there for some time. After some hours he came to, and took his bags of candies, as if nothing unusual had happened, and went to the Churva Shul.

That Shabbath, Reb Shalom's little friends noticed that their leader acted and looked different from usual. His voice was the same clear voice, but it seemed weaker. They said *Tehilim* in unison as always, after which each boy got his portion and his *Gut Shabbos* from Reb Shalom.

The children left the *shtibel*. Night closed in and the *shamash* came to lock up. He noticed the form of Reb Shalom seated at the head of the table as if he were still saying *Tehilim*. The *shamash* went to shake him to wake him. But Reb Shalom would not awaken.

"Reb Shalom, what's the matter? Are you asleep? It's time to lock up the *shul* and go home."

Reb Shalom would not move. The *shamash* became frightened and called several Jews to come and arouse the unconscious Reb Shalom. Among them was Reb Zeidel, the Yerushalmi doctor. Reb Zeidel bent over the unconscious man, felt his pulse, and looked into his eyes. Then he announced gravely. "He is dead. The *tzaddik* has gone to join his people."

That *motza'ay* Shabbath Reb Shalom was laid to rest on Har haZeithim. But his memory did not fade quickly. Though they never knew his true identity, Yerushalmim long spoke of him and remembered the gentle giant with fondness. Rav Chayim himself went to accompany the *tzaddik* upon his last journey. He recited the *kaddish* over him, too, for Reb Shalom the Gibbor had left no kin behind. It was said that he had been a man of considerable means somewhere in the diaspora, but the numerous members of his family had not allowed him to liquidate his wealth. He had left it all and gone to settle in Eretz Yisrael.

Rav Yosef Chayim Sonnenfeld even said a few words about the deceased. "Reb Shalom would surely object to our eulogizing him and praising him. Did he not labor all these years to hide his good works? But if it is forbidden to overrule his wishes, we may at least weep over him."

With the seven days of mourning were over, the kabbalists of the Beith-El Yeshiva gathered to eulogize Reb Shalom and mourn him. They dedicated a special *mincha* service in his name, reciting special kabbalistic prayers and Names in his sacred memory.

That day, the last day of *shiv'a,* a terrible cry was heard coming from near Reb Shalom's house. Three Arab corpses were removed from within, having died a strange, sudden death. These were the murderers of Reb Shalom the Gibbor.

Yerushalmim insist that the Arabs of the Old City dared do no harm to a Jew for a long time after Reb Shalom's death. After his death, as well as in his lifetime, Reb Shalom watched over his fellow Yerushalmim.

Glossary

A
alef-beith: alphabet, alphabetic
apikoress: heretic
arba kanfoth: four-cornered garment
azov ta'azov: the commandment to help someone whose burden
    is too difficult for him to carry

B
badchanim: jesters
beith din: court
beith midrash (pl. *batey midrash*): study house
beith hamikdash (pl. *batey hamikdash*): Holy Temple in Jerusalem
bima: platform
birchath ha-mazon: grace after meals
bitachon: faith
bracha: blessing
brith (mila): circumcision ceremony

C
chacham: wise
chalitza: freeing a childless widow from the obligation to marry
    her deceased husband's brother
challah (pl. *challoth*): Sabbath white bread
chazan: reader; leader of prayers
chathan: bridegroom
cheider: elementary Torah school
chevra: association
chidush (pl. *chidushim*): new interpretation
chuppa: wedding canopy

D

daven: to pray
davvening: prayer
dayan: judge
derasha: lecture

E

Eibershter: The One Above i.e., God
Eretz Yisrael: the land of Israel
erev: the evening preceding (a Sabbath or holyday)
ethrog: citron

G

gabbai: synagogue official
gaon: great rabbi
Gemara: Talmud
gemara: volume of the Talmud

H

halacha: Jewish law
Har haBayith: Temple Mount
Har haZeithim: the Mount of Olives
hesped: eulogy

K

kaddish: prayer in praise of God
kalla: bride
kethuva: marriage contract
kiddushin: marriage
kilayim: forbidden mixture
kneidlach: matzo balls
Kohein Gadol: High Priest
Kolel: institution for advanced Torah study
Kothel (*haMa'aravi*): Western Wall

L

l'chayim: toast
lulav: palm branch

M

ma'amadoth: prayers recalling the sacrifices at the Temple
ma'ariv: evening prayers

maggid: preacher
Mashiach: Messiah
maskilim: "enlightened" Jews
mathmid: one who studies Torah constantly
Me'arath haMachpeila: the Cave of Machpeila
megilla: scroll (of the Book of Esther)
mekubal (pl. *mekubalim*): kabbalist
melamed: teacher of young children
mesader: arranger
Mikdash: Holy Temple
mikveh: ritual bath
mincha: afternoon prayer
minyan (pl. *minyanim*): quorum of ten men required for communal prayer
mishlo'ach manoth: Purim gift
Mishnayoth: portions of the Mishna
mitzva (pl. *mitzvoth*): commandment
Mohel: circumciser
motza'ey: evening after
musaf: additional prayer recited on a festival
mussar: ethical lessons

N
nachas: satisfaction
netilath yadayim: ritual washing of the hands
niggun: tune
nistar (pl. *nistarim*): hidden

O
oheiv: lover of
olam haba: the world to come

P
parocheth: curtain
pasuk: Torah verse
pesak din: sentence
peyoth: sidelocks
pidyon (pl. *pidyonoth*): charity given with the hope that in its merit one will be saved from some evil

pilpul: finely reasoned lecture
poskim: authorities
pushka: charity box

R

Rabbeinu haKadosh: Our holy rabbi, used to refer to Rabbi Judah the Prince
Rav: Rabbi
rebbe: chassidic rabbi; teacher
Rechov haYehudim: Jews' Street
Ribono shel olam: Master of the universe
rosh yeshiva: head of the yeshiva

S

sandak: godfather
sechach: tree branches used for covering a sukka
sedra: the portion of the Torah read on a particular Sabbath
seifer (pl. *seforim*): Hebrew book
selichoth: penitential prayers
semicha: ordination
shaatnez: mixture of wool and linen
shacharith: morning prayer
shamash: attendant
Shass: Talmud
shechita: ritual slaughter of animals
shidduch (pl. *shidduchim*): match
shirayim: leftovers
shi'ur: lecture
shiv'a: seven days of mourning for a departed person
shochet: ritual slaughterer
shofar: ram's horn
shtender: learning stand
shtibel (pl. *shtiblach*): small synagogue
shtreimel: fur hat
shuk: market
shul: synagogue
siddur (pl. *siddurim*): prayerbook
simchah (pl. *smachoth*): happy event
sukka: booth

T

tachrichim: shroud

tallith: prayer-shawl

talmid (pl. *talmidim*): student

talmid chacham (pl. *talmidey chachamim*): Torah scholar

tashlich: ceremony of throwing one's sins into a body of water, as a metaphor of repentance

Techina: Book of Supplications

tefilla: prayer

tefillin: phylacteries

Tehillim: Psalms

teshuva: repentance

tikkun chatzoth: midnight service

tinokoth shel beith rabban: young children learning Torah

tish: table

tum'a: impurity

tzaddeikes: pious woman

tzaddik (pl. *tzaddikim*): pious man

tzitzith: fringes

V

vathikin: pious early risers

Y

yarmulka: skullcap

Yerushalmi (pl. *Yerushalmim*): resident of Jerusalem

yirath shamayim: fear of God

Yosheiv Beseither Elyon: Chapter of Psalms recited at funerals

Z

zemer: song

z"l: *zichrono leveracha*: may his memory be a blessing